Abuse Recovery

Break The Chain – Escape your Pain

By TomMc

Published by John McManus

Builder Publishing

RM12 5RA UK

Johnmc.7@live.co.uk

Dedicated to Margaret – The wind beneath my wings.

Foreword:

My initial idea for the title of this book was "Forgiving Heals the Forgiver"

As a reader you may be offended by that title; that is assuming you have been victimized or violated in some way in the past.

If you carry some extreme hatred or resentment towards someone or several people, I completely understand your disbelief that forgiving is in any way possible. In fact you may not feel that forgiving heals the forgiver in your circumstances.

You may feel that I am being patronizing by suggesting the idea.

Please bear with me and read the book with an open mind.

By the end I am confident you will be willing to give forgiveness a try.

You may come to the realization that, by forgiving you are giving yourself the gift, rather than the person you are forgiving.

You will release yourself from a burden that has been holding you back possibly for most of your life.

Most people have at one time, held a grudge or have in some extreme cases hatred in their hearts over some slight or hurt someone has done to them.

It is a terrible feeling – coldness, anger and a feeling of being betrayed. It hurts and can stick with a person for years. Because it hurts so much, the last thing one will think of is to forgive and forget.

The question is – is it hurting the person who has been responsible for the transgression as much as it hurts the victim?

Will continuing to feel unforgiving and hatred hurt the other person or will it just keep pulling the victim down and in some cases ruining their life?

Hatred, anger and frustration are emotions that affect us both mentally and physically. Those emotions are like steam building up in a kettle – unless it can escape it will blow the lid off. In other words, we will not be able to relax and lead well adjusted lives if we harbour a grudge from the past.

There are many terrible things that can and do happen in a person's life – acts sometimes perpetrated by the ones we love and trust. We can carry them for many years, not able to come to terms with trauma, hurt, anger, bitterness and many other emotions that overcome us at times when we relive the events of the past.

There is one way to ease the pain – Start to forgive!

Of course it is not easy to forgive or forget, it is much easier to carry on feeling revenge and hatred.

But are revenge and hatred doing you any good?

Are they causing any harm or stress to the one who did the wrong in the first place?

Of course not – they are completely immune to the victim's thoughts of revenge or bitterness.

But the victim's thoughts and emotions can be doing them a lot of damage – holding on to these emotions can blight a person's life and in some cases can start a depression and a complete lack of motivation possibly ruining a potentially successful life.

It is not easy to forgive, but a little bit at a time and it will get easier.

As the Chinese say "A journey of a thousand miles starts with one step"

Forgiving can start by just thinking about the problem for a few days – let the idea drift into your mind without putting up barriers.

When we forgive it has got to be without reservations - otherwise we are not forgiving and only putting our emotions at the "back of our minds" (on hold)

We have to forgive and allow ourselves to forget; otherwise, it won't work and the pain will remain.

Forgive and drive the incident/action/problem completely from your mind - then you will begin to feel good again. Every time you start to remember put it out of your mind with the thought - "I have forgiven, and it is forgotten" It can no longer hurt me.

I have forgiven, so I am now healed!

Everyone benefits from knowing their emotional needs and ways of supporting their needs and enhancing their life. Together we will uncover those ways in this book.

You are solely responsible for the consequences of using this material.

Contents

Chapter 1   8

Foundations – Can you build a foundation of confidence despite your painful experiences of abuse?

Chapter 2   45

Outlook – After "forgiveness" how does your future look?

Chapter 3   99

Reflections – What have you done about your pain and how have your actions affected you?
Chapter 4   112

Gravity – What are the seriousness and the consequences of abuse and violation experienced?
Chapter 5   126

Independence – What are your options for moving forward with your life?

Chapter 6   189

Victor or victim? Which do you want to be?

Chapter 7   253

Evolve – What will forgiving others do?

Chapter 1

Foundations – Can you build a foundation of confidence despite your painful experiences of abuse?

"Break the chain - escape your pain!!" The title of this book may leave you wondering what the chain is and how it can be broken.

The chain is the mental and emotional link you will have with the past if you have experienced abuse bullying, deception or violation in any way.

This is the chain that connects you emotionally every time you have a flash back and relive your experiences.

If you have been mistreated, abused, bullied or violated, those experiences will have left you with deeply embedded memories. Such memories wash over you and drain you of your sense of worth and the reality of the unique and truly loving and loveable person that you are.

Even small violations of our dignity will leave us feeling angry and full of resentment and most of us have felt this many times.

Abuse comes under many terms where the victims are bullied, beaten, sexually abused, emotionally abused (as in an abusive relationship or marriage) or physically deprived of food or basic comfort such as warmth.

Abuse has been rampant both in the home and in schools, colleges and care institutions for many decades.

Unfortunately this abuse has been covered up and the victims have not been afforded the proper care, counseling and in some cases not even given understanding or recognition.

I will not even begin to lay blame at the door of certain institutions or the UK's judicial system or indeed worldwide.

To review the hypocrisy and ineptitude displayed by the powers that should offer protection and justice for the victims would only serve to intensify the frustrations and anger already suffered by the thousands who have been violated.

So I will not go there!

If you are one of the many who have been mistreated and abused either emotionally, sexually or physically you are at least worthy of understanding and all possible help.

The anger, resentment, frustrating, self loathing and guilt you suffered will revisit you for many years and pull you down, sometimes to the depths of despair.

You need a painkiller to take away your pain!

My goal is to provide emotional support, as this will help in the long-term.

Trauma is another way of becoming an emotional victim. Trauma can occur in many ways; such as, assault, bereavement or contracting a serious illness.

Being conned out of our hard earned money or livelihood may cause a deep emotional imbalance.

An acrimonious separation or divorce can affect us seriously emotion wise as well as financially.

The most publicized trauma is of course suffered by soldiers on the battle front; this is known as post traumatic stress.

This type of trauma has a lasting psychological effect and may take a lot of professional help and treatment to alleviate.

Traumatic experiences will have left you with flashbacks that relive the terror and the feelings of helplessness and hopelessness that you felt at the height of your ordeal.

Your one urgent need is to dull the pain and the emotional affects caused by those flashbacks and memories.

Forgiving is the way!

Have you been bullied?

Everyone has a "weak spot" in their emotional armory; and bullies and abusers will unfortunately have an instinct about others (their victims) weak spots!

Now let me say right away that having a weak spot is no reflection on a person's character; in fact the more humane, compassionate and loving you are the more someone who is inclined to take advantage of you will see you as a weak character.

Being a person with humanity and compassion is certainly not a weakness, but must be tempered with realistic assertiveness and a display of confidence.

Humanity, compassion and love are not to be confused with being humble. If we view being humble as the opposite of arrogance then it is appropriate to be humble to a certain extent. However, being humble should not degenerate into a feeling of humiliation.

This is an example of the need to balance our emotional needs as in chapter 5.

As adults we may be perceived by potential bullies as weak and easily controlled and suppressed if we are naturally passive or if we are easily embarrassed.

There are many ways that "weak spots" can become apparent to potential predators - sometimes our body language may show ourselves as vulnerable.

I know it is not always obvious how a person is feeling from their posture but it is usually a very good indication of their emotional state.

For example when your head is bowed it is difficult to feel any euphoria.

Likewise if you want to feel good the quickest way to change your emotional state is to stand up straight, look up and smile; when you do this it is almost impossible to feel down and depressed.

Your physique also has a direct influence on your emotional state.

Moreover our "weak spot" may come from external influences at any particular moment in time.

For example we can find an oppressive employer using us to their own advantage when they perceive we are vulnerable and at their mercy due to our financial situation.

This can happen if our employer or managers are lacking in self-confidence and are trying to bolster their situation within the company by achieving an unrealistic output from their workforce.

This of course should not happen and there are many ways to address this problem.

If you find yourself in this situation it is advisable to enlist the help of a fellow worker to go with you to your manager or boss and be witness to your discussion.

You need to state clearly that you feel you are being bullied and unfairly treated.

You do not need to make any threats regarding your further actions.

Your fellow worker will stand witness to whatever you're manager or boss says in reply to your complaint.

If your mistreatment continues you are entitled to take further action. This could be to higher authority within your company or if it is the boss of the company with whom you have a problem you need to seek legal advice.

If there is authority to which the bully can be reported, this should also be done.

If you find yourself forced and bullied into doing something against you will or against your principles, it is time to summon the confidence and courage to simply say: -

"NO!"
When you are unwilling to respond to a request from someone it can be very hard to refuse with confidence.

Are you inclined to say yes even though the most logical answer is "no"?

What reasons are there to say no?

- - Can you afford it?

- -Is it out of your comfort zone?

- -Is it against your principles?

Recognize the reasons you have for saying "no" and acknowledge if they come from a lack of confidence or just a sincere disinterest in the request.

If "yes" was your answer to the request:-

- Would you be regarded as a team player?

- Would the person asking be happier?

- Would your esteem be enhanced?

Weigh up the pros and cons "Yes" or "No"!

Would the embarrassment and discomfort of saying "no" be greater than the consequences of saying "yes"?

If they are, you are advised to say "yes"!

On the other hand if you would lose too much by saying yes you should of course say "no"

You may feel guilty about saying, "no" it is not easy for most people!

In our upbringing, we are sometimes indoctrinated to say yes, but it is not always in our best interest. It is useful to recognize this and explore all situations in a balanced way.

In some situations you may feel guilty about saying, "no" to a friend, but there may be legal and moral implications for what you have been asked to do; thus placing you in an embarrassing situation. In these circumstances we should always be guided by our principles!

If a friend asked you for help and you decide to say "no" you may find they may want to push you towards a "yes".

Do not give in unless your conscience is clear.

There are many times when you gain respect by saying, "no". People who continually agree to do the extra mile are sometimes disrespected because of their meekness and servility.

I know of one person who was allocated all the extra work, including that of her colleagues, and was quite clearly being bullied; eventually she rebelled.

In fact, she gained a significantly more respect because she stood up for herself!

Standing up for yourself, means you are assertive, and you gain respect and esteem, providing you do it without aggression!

Saying, "no" without aggression takes practice and is essential.

If you find you are being victimized and expected to do more than your share, cultivate the habit of saying, "no". Make it convincing by being firm but not aggressive. Practice this habit until you become comfortable with it.

You may well ask "What has saying "no" got to do with "humanity" (See Chapter 5)

When you learn to say "no" with assertiveness, you will realize that you may have been too humble and servile in the past and that is not necessary!

It is important to maintain a balance in your life - not humble or downtrodden - just confidently assertive and and simultaneously compassionate and charitable.

Building and strengthening your self-confidence is the necessary way to combat being bullied and mistreated.

When you are very young perhaps being mistreated as a child it is almost impossible to build your confidence and this is the horror of child abuse.

As you grow older it becomes more possible to build your confidence especially if you can enlist the help of some friends or a mentor or coach.

To help you move forward with your life you will have to build on a foundation of confidence and assertiveness despite having emotional destroying experiences in your past.

What is self confidence?
To have strong self confidence you have to have positive and realistic expectations of your abilities.

You have to posses both positive and realistic expectations to nurture a proper mindset.

I have passed my driver's test and I will now buy a car and drive it on my own!

That is a positive confident statement!

I have passed my driver's test but I do not think I can drive on my own!

That is a self doubting negative statement and shows lack of confidence!

Most people are confident in at least one skill or action in their life and should take and build upon that confidence in other areas of their life.

To build your confidence, write out a list of at least 10 areas or skills in your life that you are very confident about.

You may think that 10 is a very big number of skills or competences that you are in complete confidence about, but just consider the following.

Most people are confident about:

Walking

Talking

Sitting

Standing

Reading

Writing

Using a phone

Using a knife and fork

Talking to your family

Driving a car

Cycling

Swimming

Cooking

Numeracy

House work

Gardening

Dancing

Shopping

Babysitting

Call to mind all the qualifications and skills you have learned in your life, all the experiences and all the problems you have overcome and then give yourself credit for the unique person you are.

Look at your list when it is finished and remind yourself of your capabilities - I bet you will stand much taller and have a confident look on your face when you review your list.

Now you know you are a very capable person and when you give yourself full credit you will find your confidence growing.

If there are any areas in your life you want to improve write them down and repeat "I can do this"

Keep repeating this for the next 27 days as often as you think of it and it will become embedded in your subconscious. This will compel your subconscious to keep nagging you until you achieve your goals.

The more self-confident you become, the more motivated you will be to achieve in your life.

Take as many opportunities as you can to increase your self confidence.

As you take actions that you are confident in doing you will become more aware of your abilities and credit yourself for your skills.

Transfer the confidence you have in your familiar actions into the actions that you are frightened of or feel uncomfortable with!

Many people feel uncomfortable when going for an interview or meeting new people for the first time but the confidence you feel in your familiar situations can be transferred to those occasions.

When you are confident you are in a certain state and if you become aware of that state you can then transfer it over to your uncomfortable situations.

When we meet a goal we build self-confidence.

The best strategy is to make our goals achievable in small steps. Break them down into manageable steps and as they are achieved your confidence will rapidly grow.

When you grow confidence you become less fearful and more assertive therefore able to say what you really mean.

In relationships this is very important as you may realize that your girlfriend or boyfriend or even just a friend is not doing your life any good and you need to say "no" or perhaps "goodbye".

Lack of confidence can put many people into dangerous situations where they are unable to get out of relationships and can jeopardize the rest of their lives.

Many find themselves in abusive partnerships and marriages that are ruining their lives and are lacking the confidence to break free.

Look at your life experiences and the things you have achieved despite all the handicaps that has been put your way and let yourself appreciate who you are and what you are capable of.

Get a notebook and write all your skills, all your achievements, and all the strengths that you have gained from your experiences so far.

I call this writing out your "Toolbox"

No matter what you encounter in your life, no matter how bad it seems at the time, there is always some strength that we can gain from that situation.

You are a unique human being and no matter what has happened to you; *you are capable of forgiving yourself and forgiving others!*

In this way your anguish and mental torture concerning what has happened to you will be numbed and will cease to have a devastating impact on you.

When you look at the list of your skills and achievements and your strengths then you will begin to appreciate the person you really are and to feel more confidence and self-esteem.

Doing things like this will help you to see the person you really are, not the person that your bullies and those who mistreat you have been telling you.

This is one small step towards building your confidence.

Take the necessary steps to build your confidence and ensure your future now. They do not have to be big steps-just small achievable steps.

Most people who are abused as children are abused by the very people who should be showing them love and encouragement.

It can be your parents, foster parents or teachers who sometimes misguidedly criticize the children in their care.

They think that they will force the children into changing their characters to conform to their own ideas of normality and intelligence.

This criticism will have a devastating effect on the emotional state of a child who despite all outward appearance of confidence is really a vulnerable and emotionally delicate human being.

Children may look full of confidence and bounce- ability but if continually pulled down and criticized by the people that they depend upon for care and encouragement then their confidence can drastically erode.

If you have been subjected to this kind of criticism and mistreatment then to minimize the impact on your life, consider forgiving and forgetting the incidences.

I stated above that their parents and teachers may misguidedly criticize the children in their care - criticism is a minor form of abuse but nevertheless it is very much misguided and of no benefits whatever.

Years ago (not that many years) it was known for teachers to use corporal punishment i.e. a cane to smack or "slap" children on the hands for misdeeds or for not knowing their lessons.

This had been normal procedure for perhaps centuries and it took quite a bit of modern influences to have it eradicated.

I am going to insert a story of abuse and adversity here and will go on to dwell on the many issues this story raises!

Before you read this next story I will insert a chronology of events in Frank's life:

His mother left the family home when he was a baby. He and his sister were put in care by his father and he was fostered by a middle aged Missionary and his wife who had four children of their own. His daughter was abused by a so called family friend and Frank blamed himself for not realizing what was happening. He has faced one adversity after another.

This is a real life story, but for the protection of those involved the names have been changed.

When the lilies bloom

A promise is a promise. To be absolutely honest with you, it's not a word I use very often. I suppose the most obvious and most memorable if not certainly the most important were the promises said at Barkingside registry 30 years ago almost to the day.

Of course I don't include in this the kiddies promises of my younger years, you know the promises to keep my room tidy or it wasn't me who pilfered sixpence from my foster brothers drawer, even though my hand was bright green as was the inside of my shorts pocket with an invisible dye on the coin, but once it comes into contact with the flesh something quite extraordinary happens, but I was in full denial mode, something I even to this day resort to and that word "promise" flung about willy-nilly. Did I fully understand the word? Very much like the word forgiveness which we will come to soon I promise. I knew for sure that it was wrong to break a promise, obviously, but I didn't really believe the fire and brimstone of God's wrath that my missionary foster father promised in return for my heinous deeds.

What I did learn was to expect six of the most degrading and humiliating best. His hands were hard, even sharp in places, years of carpentry turning them into shovels of calloused despair. Full on, then bare bummed over his knee to the immortal words " this is going to hurt me more than it hurts you"

I remember in a split second thinking "you're lying" "Whack"!!

I won't lie I yelled at every one, as the first sent a shockwave of absolute surprise through to my brain

24

followed by a sharp pain and then an incredible crystal clear crack echoed off my small bedroom walls (Captain Scarlet wallpaper)

Thinking back on it now, I don't think it really hurt that much, I honestly believe that the crying out and the tears were done by me to please him. As ridiculous as that sounds I think it's in my genes or something to spend my life pleasing everyone and anyone even to my detriment. I guess even at that age I was suffering from abandonment issues, and felt that if I please them they won't leave me all alone.

But that beggars the question "why steal in the first place?"

Just a brief outline of my life up to that point, I was only nine. My birth mother produced me, helped by my birth father nine months earlier, on March 21, 1962. They had already produced my sister two years earlier. Blonde hair, blue eyes, you know Shirley Temple!

I was four months old when my mom left with her sister, one of many aunties apparently, for a night of dancing. Cliché, but for me never to see her again. I can honestly say I have no spiritual, emotional or physical empathy with the lady, I am sure she didn't even have time enough to get her breasts out to feed me so I guess I was bottle fed as a baby.

Maybe that's why I've never been much of a tit man, don't hold a fascination like most of the men and some women I've come across in my sorry wretched life, fire and brimstone.

And anyway my dad and sister and I moved to London. During the day my sister and I were left at a place full of kids from one problem or another, I would wait by the gate where he would pick us up after work. And one day he just never appeared and we waited and waited and even waited some more. I didn't see my father for another 11 years.

To be fair I don't conscientiously recollect that chapter to the story but I guess at age two and a half it must have had an effect.

My sister Sandra was deeply affected, it ruined her life.

We were put up for fostering, advertised in a Christian magazine. My father a good man, just couldn't cope in those days 1964, different world. He insisted that we were to remain together.

So I guess the die was set. Unbelievably we were fostered by two late 50s returning missionaries back from Africa with four of their own loopy kids, aged 12 to 18.

To say the late 60s was a time to celebrate the future with hope and optimism is totally alien to me. It was a Dickensian life where, looking back now, everything was about the past, no change allowed. I was locked in coal cupboards, regularly hit, put down, humiliated by the monster of a man, a real life tyrant.

26

He never wanted me right from the start and it is blatantly obvious. He only wanted my sister, but we came as a couple. With Sandra getting all the cuddles and tickles??

It was mum who tried her best to shield me, but even she could only temper him, totally subservient. I crucially was taught that asking for help was a sign of weakness, something I still suffer from.............

The only person I could really talk to and give me all the support she could was my sister. There were eight people living in a small terraced house-still heated by coal, no vacuum, washing done by a copper and maybe it was the loneliest place in the world.

As then she (Sandra) was gone. I was nine years old got home from school waiting for her and like mum she never came back. They had shipped her off to a boarding school for naughty children. No warning, just gone.

So now I'm sitting here with a smarting arse trying to think what to write as promised, but I just can't stop thinking of all the wrong stuff that happened and not positives and that bloody word that crops of all time in my head thanks to a dear friend of mine, who's intellectual perspective I respect and admire, asked me if I could "forgive my wife" which he claims may "speed my recovery"

Now, I think he knew what he was doing, "here Frank take this stick and see that Hornets nest?....

Sit back and observe, maybe do a thesis.....

I was brought up having to forgive this one, that one, everyone and my life will be fruitful and happy and contented. I mean the tyrant even asked God's forgiveness before hurting himself more than he hurt me.

How can I truly forgive something that hasn't yet happened. It's on a par to "do you want a good spanking?" mmm "yesss please!!

There must be a group work for words like promise, swear..... Forgive.

Now usually I wouldn't go so far but the more I thought about forgiving my wife? the more debatable the very meaning of the word, but having never been asked for or contemplated offering forgiveness, thought I'd give it a go.

First stop my trusted Chambers 20th century dictionary:

forgive, to pardon, overlook, to remit a debt or offence.

Forgiveness, disposition to pardon.

Now the first problem is that I was taught the only one capable of granting pardon was God that my tyrant believed in (good enough for me not to believe). What these religious worshippers don't realize that God doesn't actually exist when you pray you basically pray to yourself because the "God" if you like is really your inner self.

For someone who doesn't believe I certainly ask him for help when needed, bribe him even curse him, but I'm only castigating myself.

What is there to forgive? If I forgive what benefit will that do.

Sheila, I forgive you for treating me like a doormat, mentally using me, driving Lynne away, dumping me, when I most needed help, because I was surplus to requirements, for leaving me alone in a hell she couldn't understand. For telling me during normal conversation that "I only married you to spite my father but I kinda grew to love you", set me up in front of the twins with the police and degradation that followed, who eight weeks into 12 week rehab informs me I can't return home and she would get me arrested if I tried - "in the middle of rehab?"

For some sick reason she decided it would be in the best interests to aid my recovery, part of my convalescence maybe, to sit at my hospital bed after (me) spending two weeks in, contacting pneumonia and being told by all the doctors that she should call the family in because when they turn the life support off they didn't expect me to survive as all my major organs had ceased working. After all that alone a couple of weeks later (me) having to learn to talk she calmly tells me that while they (the children) were praying each day for me "I was hoping you would die cause it would pay the mortgage and I wouldn't have to worry about bills anymore, now you haven't I'm sort of "pleased"

Before carrying on are we talking about collective forgiveness or forgiveness for individuals?

Did I tell you the one about after some weeks me query why my real father hadn't called maybe even visited me bearing in mind I had actually died five times to be told "oh I didn't inform him, why would I? "We're separated"

I didn't die for Christ sake. "I wasn't sure you would have wanted me to"

All of this behavior I allowed to happen. I had choices, by forgiving her for treating me this way makes me out to be weak, pathetic even.

Why did I allow, put up with it, why didn't I just leave. I thought long and hard about this. Maybe I just cocooned myself in some kind of safety net. It was easier, or maybe I just loved her. There's not a lot of difference between a woman who doesn't leave an abusive relationship and a man who is emotionally abused. Is there?

When, after we had discovered the sexual abuse of our daughter Lynne (by a family friend) things deteriorated. Once Sheila started courses in counseling I felt like I was being analyzed, if I wanted to talk about anything troubling me, she used to snap at me that she couldn't be my counselor or she couldn't be my mother? When the truth was in reality she couldn't actually be my wife.

I became over time, what I call a functioning alcoholic. Not overnight but gradually self-medicating, so terribly lonely. I still held down a job and coped with the house, never falling down drunk.

Anyway, after my brush with anal searches and my humiliating set up, I found myself in a room at the Courtney in Manor Park right by the city of London cemetery, and my life plummeted into a deep depression.

I was honestly trying to kill myself with alcohol abuse, I just lost the plot, lost everything I had ever held dear to my life and I wallowed in self-pity, blamed myself for everything. Not good, I honestly drank myself unconscious day after day hoping I wouldn't wake up in the morning, I couldn't even do that properly.

The day I met my guardian angel changed everything. She was from housing and her name was Violet Easton. I can honestly say that her genuine sympathy seem to snap me out of myself. Someone had found me and showed sincere concern for my well-being.

I started to revisit RDAS. I had decided the only way to beat the booze was if I could attend a residential detox followed immediately by residential rehab. I knew that community rehab wouldn't work and took nine whole months of living in drunken squalor, didn't eat for days on end, getting more and more depressed and self destructive. Finally I got my break and on 8th September 2013 I went into detox at Craig House

Canary Wharf followed by my 12 week residential rehab at Oak Lodge Putney.

I will sit down and write about this time in more detail on another date. Suffice to say that on my first day of detox my key worker at RDAS left, leaving me with no outside contact.

At eight weeks into rehab I had the phone call saying there was no chance of reconciliation and at nine weeks my key worker in rehab had a massive and quite spectacular nervous breakdown whilst in a group session. When I had my one on ones with him he used to be close to tears at the end of each session. Very peculiar, and it wasn't till 10 weeks in that I was finally offered an extra six weeks at Oak Lodge.

I don't claim to understand what follows. One week before leaving Oak Lodge I received a letter from Redbridge council housing department ordered me to report at Clements Road office as I was officially classed as homeless and they will decide then what to do with me. So much time spent on other things than what I should have been working on. Nine am. I had to report from Putney.

Out in the big wide world unshackled but not free.

I find it inconceivable that Redbridge would pay out £900 per week for 18 weeks £16,200 to then only (me) being dumped quite literally in a box in Plaistow. Once again back above another off-license.

There was no thought put into my continued abstinence. No support, totally alone.

It was seven at night when I was deposited in Plastow. I had absolutely no idea of my whereabouts. I remember the feeling of helplessness, and downright negativity mixed with anger, deep depression. For three days I was drinking before being rushed into hospital with abdominal problems. Once again my Guardian Angel Violet Easton appeared and give me all the encouragement she could but I had some sort of breakdown and she quickly got me transferred to Jason Leigh house!

I just can't fully put into words how Lou saved me by offering me a place.

How ironic, coming from a house with boundaries and structure with discipline and encouragement to a house full of street drinkers actively drinking, you couldn't make it up, the feeling of abandonment was quite intense.

RDAS passed me to WDP who after I had been abstaining for six weeks severed their contact with me.

The first three weeks though really seem to work for me ("more luck than judgment, but I'll take any luck that comes my way "albeit a valuable rarity")

The sight and sound of the majority of the house actually keep me away from the drink, my neck was to be scammed again, an appointment with the

Psychologist and a new GP who appeared uninterested in me.

So is this what it feels like to turn a corner. I felt excited and hopeful for the future, attentive staff, which are sympathetic to my needs, there to support me, looking up.

Oh!! Frank, Frank, Frank , when will you ever learn. For every good action there must be an equal if not greater bad reaction even so, cardiac arrest X4, I never saw that coming.

Back in the black bottomless pit prepared yet again to claw and scrambled back, I'm getting there, the only problem is I don't know where there is, will I know when I get there?

Anyway forgive me for I digress, let's talk forgiveness. I can only speak for myself as it is wholly personal, unique to the individual. I couldn't possibly ask someone else to forgive someone other than me even me to offer myself to be forgiven doesn't take it as a cert that I will be forgiven, as I have said before it means I have to admit a guilt which deserves to be forgiven and for me to forgive they have to admit their guilt otherwise what are you forgiving?

With Sheila I can see she knows no better, it's her upbringing, but is she guilty? Ignorant?

I still maintain I had some choice. Would it make me feel better if I forgive her?

I don't think so. Anyway its fuel for the fire in my belly, so long as it's under control it's good to have a fire in your belly. Would I change anything? Probably but then one tiny little change will have massive connotations, pebble dropped in lake effect, life changing!

I'm not proud of where I am in life, but I'm certainly proud of the way I have held myself in adversity. Do I forgive anybody? Not really.

Would I ask for forgiveness??

Maybe when the Lilies Bloom.

Frank has raised a lot of very deep emotional concerns that are troubling him about "Forgiveness"

I consider that it would be totally remiss of me if I neglected to address the issues in Frank's story.

Frank has major concerns about forgiving, one being the fact that if he does not forgive he will still have the *"fire in his belly"* and this fire he perceives as being a motivation to him to keep going.

This fire is of course a sense of anger, resentment and even guilt for allowing himself to be ill treated in such a manner.

This relates to his last period of deception and betrayal by his wife, not only from his first abuse as a child.

Those emotions are ones that most men will have in the same circumstances because men over many thousands of years have grown pride in the fact that they are responsible for the protection and well-being of their family.

Because of this men especially will feel it very hard to let go of the anger and resentment towards anyone either within the family or outside of it, which has transgressed or violated them (or their family).

Despite the fact that most people who have been abused or betrayed, have been unable either physically or emotionally to counteract the abuse, they will still feel guilty and perhaps angry with themselves for allowing the abuse to take place.

This is futile and only adds to the effects of the abuse as it repeatedly visits them emotionally despite the fact that it (the abuse) has long since ceased.

The past can never be undone and harbouring anger and resentment will only damage the person with the anger and not the perpetrator of the violation.

Anger breeds stress that acts on us physically by producing harmful chemicals in our brain that acts on our body and lowers our immune system.

Not only do we damage ourselves emotionally by continuing to relive the trauma of past violations and hurts, those emotional thoughts can lead to lowering of our immune systems and leave us susceptible to disease.

The act of "forgiveness" will diminish the intensity of the emotional flashbacks from violation and take away their power.

"Forgiveness" does not mean that the forgiver is condoning or taking away the guilt of his or her abuser, violator or betrayer.

Forgiveness is for one's own benefit - not for the benefit of the person you are forgiving.

It takes a lot of soul-searching, a lot of humanity and a lot of deep down courage to forgive.

The courage is needed when a victim looks inwards and asks "have I got the strength and the flame to go on with my life without the driving force of hatred and resentment"

Can I replace it with the strength of "Love" - especially love for myself?

Love is one of the essential motivational needs that all humans have! (See chapter5).

Just consider the difference between living a life of love and living a life of anger, hatred and resentment!?

The choice is obvious!

A more devastating and completely abhorrent abuse is of course sexual abuse.

Sexual abuse to a child or indeed to anyone, to my mind is the most despicable thing anyone can do to another human apart from murder.

The trauma and humiliation inflicted upon this innocent victim usually has a lifelong mental impact.

This emotional impact affects the victim; depriving them of confidence and self-esteem and in some cases causing depression and lack of progress in life.

Bullying and intimation in your teens and young adulthood has a devastating effect on ones confidence and emotional stability.

If you are in your teens be aware of the following events with your peers or your boy/girl friends.

Warning to teenagers and young adults!
Unfortunately, potential abusers don't have a warning tattooed on their foreheads.

In fact, they often seem charismatic, popular and attentive at first. Outsiders can think the abuser is great, as they rarely show their destructive behaviour in public. This can make it even harder for the victim to ask for help.

Check out our seven signs of abusive behaviour to see if you should be worried:

1 Isolation.

Your boyfriend or girlfriend tries to break up your friendships and keeps you away from family.

This can include constantly checking texts and emails, stopping you from using your phone

2 Control.

They tell you what to wear, who to hang out with, what to spend your money on and even what to say.

They get very angry if you do not respond to texts immediately.

If you try to break up with them, they may threaten to self-harm or to harm you.

3 Humiliation.

This involves putting you down in front of people, calling you names, saying that you are no good at things, or that you are ugly and no one else would fancy you.

4 Explosive anger.

They can switch from being nice to extreme anger and rage at the slightest thing. You cannot win and you feel like you are walking on egg shells.

5 Blame.

They blame you for making them behave in an abusive way. They may also blame other people for their problems or feelings.

6 Excuses.

You try to find excuses for the way your boyfriend or girlfriend behaves because you don't want others to think badly of them.

7 Pressure to have sex.

They may put pressure on you to have sex or do things that you're not ready for. You should never feel pressurized to have sex in a relationship. It is not acceptable for a partner to make you feel bad or call you names because you do not want sex. Remember, it is illegal to have sex in the UK if you are under 16, or in Ireland if you're under 17.

By kind permission

http://www.faceup.ie

In 1991, boxer Michael Watson collapsed at the end of his World Championship super-middleweight fight with Chris Eubank. He was in a coma for 40 days, and a blood clot in his brain left him partially paralysed. In 2003 he completed the London Marathon, six days after he set out. On the final leg he was accompanied by Chris Eubank. He has written a book about his experience:

Michael Watson's Story: The Biggest Fight

Before the accident I was not a committed Christian. I believed but I was too busy, rushing this way and that, with no time to reflect. Yet I was a loveable person in society and I was doing well. My ultimate goal was to be World Champion.

After the accident it took me a long time to face up to reality. One minute I was a top celebrity, in the ring going for the ultimate prize. The next minute, blank... I woke up in a hospital ward with strange people all around me. I was totally confused and terribly frustrated.
Before my accident, even though I believed in God I didn't go to Church because it didn't suit my image.

I was too wrapped up in the pleasures of the world - fast cars, expensive clothes, girls. But from the moment I regained consciousness in hospital I took refuge in God.

I prayed for strength, and I prayed for Chris Eubank. I knew he was suffering. If you've got a heart - and he has - you can never be the same after something like this happens. I didn't feel any anger toward him because it could have happened either way. You have to let bygones be bygones. Getting angry won't correct the past. Instead, I knew I had to concentrate on the future and look to starting a new life. If I had animosity about what Chris had done to me, I'd be breaking myself down mentally as well as physically. How could I then move on?

Instead I became closer to God and found inner peace and strength. I needed to be still for a time. Now I feel brand new. I love the way I am because I've got a lot of love in my heart. I feel even better than I did before.

Of course, there are also times when I feel discouraged and depressed, but then friends come round and make me laugh and put joy back into my heart. I couldn't have got this far without my friends and my family.

Certainly I believe in the concept of forgiveness. It is always better to give than to receive. I'd like to think I'd feel the same if my injuries were the result of a vicious attack. Jesus is my inspiration. Christian or not, how can you fail to be moved by the words of Jesus on the cross: "Father, forgive them, for they know not what they do".

The above story has been republished by kind permission of the "Forgiveness Project" www.theforgivenessproject.com

What's crucial to resolve in your life right now?

TomMc Abuse recovery coach

http://tinyurl.com/j34asab

http://www.tommcabuserecoverycoach.co.uk

Chapter 2

Outlook - After "forgiveness" how does your future look?

When we are mistreated and abused our dignity and sense of self-respect is shattered and we are made to feel vulnerable and helpless.

Abusers are experts at using emotional weaknesses to inflict pain and humiliation on their victims.

Victims of abuse are usually children who have not yet developed the strong confidence and wisdom to disregard their tormentor's vile words and actions.

As children our natural emotional needs predominantly are to be loved and respected.

The emotional impact of being abused mistreated and neglected as a child is almost impossible to explain; or indeed understand or visualize by anyone who has not experienced such abuse.

When we are disrespected our confidence plummets and we feel humiliated, helpless and worthless.

In extremes cases victims can feel guilty for the abuse they are suffering.

In long-term matrimonial or partnership abuse the victim will sometimes cover up for the abuser as a result of a misguided sense of guilt and loyalty.

In such circumstances, the abuser will always have an explanation and reason for their actions. This reason always places blame on the victim, regardless of how unreasonable this may seem.

Abusers in a partnership or marriage situation are usually manipulative and controlling. They will explain their actions in such a way that it will almost seem reasonable to all outward appearance.

These abusers usually suffer from lack of confidence and many cases are suffering with depression.

They can be experts at lying and scheming in order to portray their actions as reasonable to everyone else; yet simultaneously, they exert cruel emotional torture on their partners.

A word of caution here - it has been known for victims to escape an abusive partnership and promptly join up with the next bully that they meet; be it male or female.

Being a victim of abuse will at least result in a deep feeling of anger, resentment and in some cases the desire for revenge!

This can result in depression and a deep sense of helplessness and the inability to be motivated in any direction.

Indeed your outlook will appear very bleak and it will take great effort to bounce back to a normal state of mind.

Forgiveness will dull the anger and resentment that has driven you to this state of anxiety and feelings of being stuck in a state of limbo.

Anxiety is part of depression and we will explore how to manage anxiety and stress.

Can you manage your anxiety and stress?
Your emotions play a major role in your state of health and well-being. When you are beset by stress and anxiety, your physical health will suffer and your immune system will be weakened leaving you susceptible to illnesses.

Your brain controls your body, but when it is not functioning fully, it impounds upon your body's ability to protect itself.

Anxiety and stress are two emotions felt as a result of fear. Fear is both good and bad for us. It is good, because it enables us to understand danger.

It is bad because if we allow it, it can paralyze us and stop us from taking the action that we need to function properly.

We become anxious and stressed when we fear something in the present moment or something that we anticipate happening in the future.

This fear and worry releases many hormones that inhibits our body from working properly and lowers our resistance to disease and injury. Fear also releases chemicals in the muscles, which become toxic if they are not used.

Stress and anxiety can also lead to hypertension, (high blood pressure) which can subsequently contribute to heart problems such as angina.

Stress and worry are common problems in modern life and many techniques have been developed to counteract them.

Stress management through time management!
One of the causes of stress in the modern-day work environment is the pressure to meet deadlines.

When you are given a work deadline you are put under pressure and will feel stressed, not knowing for sure whether or not you will be able to meet it.

Unless you are very positive minded you will be anxious in case you encounter a problem that will hinder your ability to complete the task on time.

This of course will cause you to become stressed.

When you are feeling stressed you will be unable to relax, concentrate fully and work to your full potential.

You will be aware that you are not working at your full speed and this in turn will heighten your stress; thus creating a Catch-22 situation unless you are able to find a way to break the circle.

To manage your time you have to discipline yourself to take a few minutes to review your overall job or task and plan how you are going to do it. When you have your plan in place, you will begin to feel more confident about your ability to meet the deadline.

This will lower your stress level and help you become more efficient.

When you are stressed out you will spend too much time worrying and not enough time planning your strategy.

A good strategy is to become more aware of how you think about your success in everything that you do.

Many people are better saying what they do not want rather than what they do want! Consequently most people will get what they do not want instead of what they have been longing for.

The simple fact is that whatever you set your mind upon you will invariably achieve it.

So if you set your mind on what you do not want then "bingo" you will get it!

A little story comes to mind - a teacher says to her pupils "If I tell you not to think about a green giraffe - what is the first thing you will think of?

A green giraffe!

So do not think of what you do not want, think of what you do want and as everything in your life begins with a thought. This then becomes a plan, then an action and finally reality!

A man I know very well told me this story:

My daughter was caught smoking at school by her teacher. I was called for an interview with the teacher along with my daughter. As we approached the school I said:

"Now it is up to you whether you want to smoke or not but do not get caught, having me come in to be interviewed by the teacher"

(he did not really want her to be smoking but he was being devious, knowing that if he showed he was upset by her smoking she might through sheer teenage rebelliousness continue to smoke)

She said "Dad I will not get caught again because I will not smoke again"

She did not get caught again and she did not smoke again simply because she said "I will not get caught and I will not smoke".

When you put your statements in positive language you will be successful. In fact she is still a non-smoker!

When you set your mind on your goal your subconscious will guide you towards it and you will automatically start planning for what you want.

It is very important to have a clear picture in your mind of what you really want and to be exact as to the quantity is (money) or shape, size or form of what you want. Such knowledge will help you achieve your goals.

To be a success you must know exactly what you want and have the mindset that you will get it.

Visualize how you are going to feel when you get what you want, how it is going to look, how it sounds (when you passed your driver's test, how the car will sound when you are driving it) and what people are going to say when you get what you want.

When you reach your goal what will it do for you? Will it enhance your esteem in your community or family, will it make you richer, will it make you more employable and raise your standard of living?

Think of all the good things that will come your way when you reach your goals!

Write down your goals and put a time limit on them. Always set a date for reaching each stage or step towards your goal! Read them often and review your progress each week.

A good way to help you succeed is to employ the help of a progress mentor who will keep you motivated and on target.

http://tinyurl.com/j34asab (TomMc ARC)

Having joy and laughter in your life!

If you suffer from anxiety and stress suggesting that you have joy and laughter in your life may sound condescending.

However, if you can put aside your worries and fears for a few minutes, think back to the last time you were really happy, visualize what happened and how you felt a surge of happiness.

Run the memory like a video in your mind and see it in brilliant colour, larger than life and hear all the sounds associated with the recollection.

You will find that the larger and brighter you make the video, the more joy you will elicit from your memory.

Practice this whenever you feel anxious or stressed. Good memories and good feelings trigger a flow of endorphins to our brain and help relieve our stress and worry.

The more frequent you do this the more your brain will desire it and soon you will be able to reject your feelings of stress and worry.

It is human nature to pursue pleasure and avoid pain, therefore if you can provide pleasure instead of pain (worry and anxiety) your brain will like it and it will quickly become a habit.

Try this as a stress management technique!

"Early to bed and early to rise makes a man healthy wealthy and wise!"

(I do not know where that came from, but I am sure I have heard it thousands of times; it is probably Irish.)

I must admit that I am not the tidiest of people and it may sound hypocritical for me to suggest that the state of your room influence your willingness to get up early in the morning.

If you are sleeping in a pleasant room, nicely decorated and with the right temperature and ventilation you will be better prepared to wake up energized and ready for the day's activities.

Plan an exciting event for the day ahead and you will have a reason for getting out of bed.

When you plan something that is in line with your passion be it a sporting activity or your favorite hobby, then life will be that much more interesting and joyful.

By waking up early you will achieve much better health and have more time to spend on activities you enjoy. In addition your productivity will be enhanced.

When you become accustomed to going to bed early you will find that you will have much better sleep and it will be much easier to wake without feeling stressed.

Some people get into a habit of going to bed very late, perhaps watching a late-night movie or reading a book, completely forgetting about the time.

This does not promote a full night's sleep each night, the recommended period of sleep according to research.

Lack of proper sleep will heighten your stress and worry as relaxation and having proper rest are vital to both our emotional and physical well-being.

When you are well rested and have a reserve of stamina it is much easier to combat feelings of worry and anxiety.

A peaceful night's rest is much easier when you have not been stressed out by trying to reach a strict deadline, so you will have to look at time management and work out a way to break the "deadlines" - Catch-22 situation.

If you have any unresolved problems now is the time to work out a solution and assure yourself that everything is going to be okay.

Do this before you go to bed.

Always remember that it is our nature to "make mountains out of mole hills" in other words to view our problems as much larger than they are.

Look at your problems like a video in your mind and reduced it to a small picture receding into the distance.

You have heard it said "out of sight out of mind" and there is much truth in this.

Plan ahead, relax and visualize a successful outcome to your job, therefore breaking the spiraling circle that anxiety and stress have caught you up in.

To help you wake up early you can think of the benefits and rewards attached to the extra energy that you will feel. Energy is a great force against anxiety, as it is difficult to feel anxious when your energy is high.

There is a big downside to waking up late as you will open up lot of difficult situations for yourself at work, at play or with your friends and colleagues, indeed you may have let them down and proven that you are unreliable.

This again will provide more ammunition for your stress and anxiety as you will now feel you are letting yourself down and losing self-esteem.

Relax, get proper sleep, view your problems realistically, manage your time, plan your day ahead and visualize your success - those are some of the ways you can manage your stress and anxiety.

Carrying the emotional load from past experiences is a burden that will continue to drag you down and can cause you to question where your life is going and what is the point?

When you get to this point it is time to stop and realize that everyone has a part to play in this universe.

We are all unique individuals and worthy of being loved and respected.

We may not think that we have anything to offer or are capable of making a difference to anyone's life or our own.

This is completely the wrong way of thinking as we were all put on this planet to make a difference and be part of the universe.

Everyone has a part to play however small or big.

Each one of us has an impact on everyone we meet every day that we live and that impact may be life changing although we do not know that!

You may give one word of encouragement and support to a fellow human that can completely change a terrible life into one that is full of richness and joyfulness.

When you look at the potential good even the weakest of us can do for others and for ourselves it is amazing.

"What you do and wish for others you do and wish for yourself!"
I truly believe that quotation.

I know many people who have been really down, chin on the ground and could not figure out how to raise them up. A few short days later they have a smile on their face and feel quite good.

What did they do?

1. They forgave themselves and others!
2. They started to help and support others!
3. They realized that they could have a future and visualized it!

The first and most important step is to forgive yourself and anybody else who has wronged you, and forgive them unconditionally.

Unconditionally means that you do not hold anger or revenge towards yourself or that person in your heart.

When you do this you will find that the memories have lost their ability to hurt or drag you down as they have done in the past.

Just imagine the great feeling and release that would be!

When you look to the future, you will realize that your outlook is not as bleak as you thought before you gave "forgiveness" a try!

To help us look at a future in a realistic manner it is useful to be open to the idea of setting goals.

Setting goals enables us to become more motivated and realistic about our possibilities in the future.

It also helps us change our mindset and our emotional state in life.

Change must be slow because if it is too fast you can expect to go back to your old self and to your old beliefs no matter how those beliefs and attitudes were holding you back.

Let us look at dolphin training. Trainers motivate the dolphins to do tricks by rewarding them for a job well done. The ones who do not perform properly are ignored.

This works brilliantly with people because when we are rewarded we feel good and happy so we will tend to do our best in order to get recognition and praise.

We also feel hurt, and our self esteem is dragged down when we are ignored.

If you are pleased with how someone is acting towards you, reward them with a smile and perhaps a word of thanks, this will help them to continue acting the way you would like them to.

On the other hand if they are ignoring you and being nasty and you cannot get them to change their attitude just simply ignore them.

Change does not happen instantly it can sometimes be slow, but you will need patience. When change happens slowly, it tends to be more permanent.

You may tend to get upset and angry if a person does not change their attitude and be more civil towards; you will only make the situation worse if you lash out verbally or worse still physically at anybody.

If a friend has upset you in any way try talking calmly to them and explain how you feel. Quite often our friends do not realize that they are upsetting us and are willing to make amends.

A calm discussion and explaining your understanding of the situation will be to your advantage.

If calm discussion does not clear the situation; it may be best to let matters rest.

Review the problem after a few days when all parties have calmed down.

In life you will have gained experiences, skills, knowledge and will no doubt possess many talents that you can use, I call this your "Toolbox".

Now you can realistically look at what tools you have and decide what goals you are equipped to achieve.

When I say a realistic look, I mean do not underestimate your talents and skills or your experience.

I remembered about 20 years ago, when asked to state my capabilities, and skills I wrote only two, or three! I felt that I would be boasting if I claimed more!

I now know better - we should always give ourselves due credit for what we have in our "Toolbox".

In fact not only the tools you have, but more importantly the interests, hobbies and passions that you have. Whatever goals or path in life you choose, you must have passion for it or you are doomed to failure.

Not only are you likely to fail, but if you are trapped in a job or career that does not coincide with your passion you will feel like a prisoner for the rest of your life.

Yes, there are millions in the world like that!

Is your understanding of your strengths and values the key to finding your passion?

Knowing the strengths of your confidence and self-esteem will assist you in deciding your true passion!

Most people, as they grow up will develop interest in sports or a particular skill or pursuit that they find interesting and enjoyable.

It may be a sport or skill that is unique to them or it may be interactive. Whatever it is it can develop into a passion for the rest of their life, which if carried over to their work environment will prove a most fulfilling pleasure.

A passion is what you are keen on, what your interest lie in, be it a hobby or a skill, anything in fact that makes you feel fulfilled and happy in your life.

It will be something that fits comfortably within your educational and physical capabilities. Your passion will also have to sit comfortably with your principles and beliefs.

If your chosen passion does not fit the above criteria you will not feel satisfied or fulfilled.

You may have a passion for some sport as a follower or as a participant, or some hobby that gives you great satisfaction. Your hobbies and interests are usually in line with your strength's, your skills and your education.

Those are all things that you can adopt as your passion and in fact when working at or engaged in whatever your passion is you are sure to be successful and to feel fulfilled in your life.

Below are some strengths you can search for within yourself:

Belief (in yourself)

Confidence

Desire

Discipline

Patience

Persistence

Philanthropy

Respectability

Tolerance

Vision

Principles:

Honesty

Humanity

Values:
Your family

Your health

Your home

Your values may change over time, but most of our deep-set principles remain throughout our lives.

Your values comprise what you consider good and worth nourishing, acting upon and sustaining in your life.

It is important that your career is in true alignment with your passions and interests otherwise you are doomed to a life of mediocrity and frustration.

To reach your true potential and become successful you have got to be in a career that is in true alignment with your passion, your unique personality and the person that you truly are.

When you do things naturally, without great effort, getting great pleasure from them, those are the things and activities that you should consider choosing as your career or work passion.

You will love your career and your life and you will feel confident and powerful in your chosen activity.

When your job is your passion and you are passionate about your job you will find it so much easier to jump out of bed in the morning, looking forward with happy anticipation to your day's work ahead.

This is one of the huge benefits of working within an area that you are interested in and get fulfillment from whatever that area is.

When you consider most career people like teachers, doctors, nurses, veterinary practitioners who are following their chosen passion, are blessed with a feeling of accomplishment, fulfillment and pleasure in their work, it is easy to see that there are great advantages to choosing a career that is in line with your interests and passion.

You will experience a heightened motivation, stronger confidence in your required skills, enhanced self-esteem, and a much happier and contented life.

You will also find is much easier to be focused and be more efficient at work as you will not be finding it boring or repetitive.

With a happier and contented life, you will be experiencing much better health due to lack of stress.

If your career or job is not in line with your passion, you may well feel trapped unfulfilled and have a feeling that you are going to prison instead of a job each day.

This is not the way to live, as we should all be free spirits and work within our sphere of interests not just to make a living because it is necessary, but to lead lives of fulfillment.

When you meet friends who are continually looking forward to the holidays and continually moan about their work, then you will understand that they have created a prison for themselves by choosing the wrong career.

If you ever consider changing your job, review your strengths, your principles, your values and the interest's in life that gives you pleasure when considering a change of job or career.

Research the company that you are seeking a job with and ensure that their company values and ethos are in line with your passion.

When you find your passion you are not guaranteed an easy life, but you will feel it much easier to lead a richer life spiritually and materially as you will not be feeling frustrated or bored and it will be much easier to keep your mind activated.

You will find much more pleasure in life and it will be easier to be positive and motivated in all things you do when you are following your true passion.

When you are following your passion you are reflecting the person you are in what you do. You will feel yourself more respected and valued when you are working in an environment and a job that fits into your life's passion and interests.

You will feel more true to yourself, be happier and be very much confident in everything you do because you know you are following a path that is in alignment with your strengths, your beliefs, values and principles.

Some people, although quite successful in the career may feel extremely unfulfilled and almost quite depressed by times, because the career they are following lacks interest for them even when the salary is extremely high.

You may read quite often about very successful people, celebrities, footballers, world famous athletes, who although extremely successful in their field are still quite unhappy with their life.

Those people are missing out on having a fulfilling passion in their lives and just cannot get fulfillment from what they are doing.

Many people go through life just performing the motions and getting no real satisfaction out of what they are doing, sometimes doing a repetitive job for their complete lifetime.

Only when they retire and perhaps take up some voluntary work do they really find a fulfilling job.

To spend all your lifetime in a job that you do not love is a catastrophe.

You only get one lifetime, make the best possible use of it!

You may wonder when you hear your friends talking about stress, worry and having sleepless nights what is causing it all.

Is it because they are in a monotonous soul destroying job and if they change to a job in line with their passion their health and happiness will benefit?

Not alone does the fact that you may be engaged in a job that is not your passion, but if your boss is in a job that he feels is not his passion, he may very well take out his frustration on you and on your fellow workers.

We wonder why so many bosses are bullies?

It is quite possible that they have chosen the wrong job, or at least a job that they are not confident in and therefore will try to blame everybody else for their own shortcomings.

If you are in charge of a workforce and you feel yourself being frustrated, give due consideration as to whether you are in the right job or not.

An enormous amount of problems are created by trying to fit square pegs into round holes!

Remember we only get one life in this world so if you consider yourself a square peg do not try to fit into a round hole - instead find a job that is in line with your passion and reap the benefits.

Your mindset will play a strong part in how you control your state in life.

How is your mindset?

Your mindset is your subconscious formulated by all the experiences you've had, and all the beliefs and principles that you have cultivated during your life.

If your environment and the beliefs you have been taught are not enabling you to go forward in life then you have the wrong mindset.

If you do not believe, you are a skilled person and capable of achievement in your life then you need to reset your mindset.

You need to wipe out such belief because we are all capable of our own way of achieving and reaching our full potential.

If you consider that you have not had the full educational benefits to make you successful then you should stop and look around at the people who are extremely successful.

Some of them, in fact, have had poor education and have beaten their way up in the world despite what most people would consider being handicapped education wise.

You may have certain limitations set in your mind about what you can do and what you cannot do and the tasks you are happy to undertake. Within these limits, you may be happy to carry on your life but unless you leave your comfort zone you may find it very hard to advance.

Leaving your comfort zone can be very uncomfortable, and you may face embarrassment and fear of the unknown.

You may be unwilling to go further because you are facing the unknown and would rather stay safely within your comfort zone.

When your comforts zone is limited, you will be hard to motivate.

When a new idea or experience presents itself, you will be likely to check to see if it is in your comfort zone and if it is not you would be reluctant to embark upon it.

This is unfortunate because it would restrict your progress and stop you from achieving the success you deserve.

One of the emotional needs of man is "Growth" and if you do not embark upon new experiences you will miss out on "Growth".

Growth is not just a physical thing it is growing in the mind as well and expanding your mental faculties. This is important for all human beings because unless we keep the brain exercised we become bored and lose motivation, quite possibly becoming depressed.

To be successful, you have to live outside your comfort zone.

Remember anything you do in this life, if it is not a pleasure and fulfilling, then the time you have spent on it will be wasted and you will never get it back again - you only live once!

If you job or your career is not what you wanted it to be you will find it is much more difficult to make the proper decisions and to be persistently efficient in what you are doing.

If you are bored with your job or unhappy with the situation at work then you will not be efficient and because you are not efficient your job will be more and more difficult and less and less pleasure.

Is your personality reflected in your work?

Are you an outgoing person?

If you are, are you in a supportive role within your job or is your job a supporting role to other people.

By this I mean do you have a healthcare, educational or volunteering role?

You may be artistic, visual and be able to see the world in full colour and perhaps are working in a dreary repetitive job where you are not really producing; it will be very easy to understand if you are feeling frustrated and unfulfilled.

Perhaps you have an unfulfilled dream, but because you fear to step out of your comfort zone or failing to support yourself and others within your care, you have put your dream on the backburner and deprived yourself of the opportunity to be happy and fulfilled.

In previous chapters I have touched on the problem of fear and how it curtails us.

Do not let fear be your governor - take responsibility, be the creator of your destination!

Live your dream!

Millions in the this world pursue a career path that they are not in love with, simply because it looks secure, and they choose it instead of following their dream, in the hope that they will be financially secure rather than going after what they want!

Whatever career you choose, find someone, who is successful in that field or profession, to model, in order to be successful yourself. Modeling successful people is a recognized way to becoming successful yourself.

Now be aware that I am not advising you to change your job just for the sake of changing, especially if you are not financially secure and you might be putting yourself in danger of unemployment.

Again, if you are not 100% certain of your skills even within your passion you can always enhance your capabilities by going to college part-time or doing a home study course. An easily achievable task and whatever you learn will benefit you.

Be ready for all opportunities and possibilities that life may present to you!

Quite often you may find that you will stumble upon a job that becomes your passion quite by chance. A few years ago I became redundant and someone I knew guided me towards a job in a homeless shelter. This job became the most fulfilling of my life!

Admittedly, it was way down the scale moneywise but I experienced enormous fulfillment in working at the shelter.

To me the most fulfilling moments of my life have been when I supported other people in whatever way possible and I get great personal happiness and pleasure when I see someone move forward in his or her life.

I have found that through the years the only true satisfaction comes from "giving"

Not from "taking"!

One of my personal quotations is:

"You have to give, before you get!"

Be constantly on the alert for something new; your success can be on the next bend of the road.

Just follow your heart and passion!

Following your passion does not always guarantee success; hard work will be necessary for achieving your dreams.

When you are following your passion, then you will naturally have more knowledge of what you are doing and more skills to lay claim to; Moreover you will also love your job, making life more pleasure, less stressful and, therefore, you much healthier.

Success will also come much easier.

Success is being happy and content with the financial, physical and spiritual state you are in at the present!

To be cheerful, smile and laugh as often as possible;

To have the respect of intelligent and wise people and the affection of all within your relationships;

To have an honest appreciation of constructive criticism and be able to endure the treachery of false friends;

To appreciate beauty everywhere and to recognize the best traits in others;

To ensure you leave the world a better place, whether by a healthy family, a garden plot or by contributing to the social condition of your fellow humans.

To make someone richer by the fact that you have touched that person by sharing the unique talents and gifts of which you are endowed!

This is the way to be a success!

Being wealthy does not always equate to success. Happiness can mean much more than wealth; certainly being healthy should be more important than being wealthy.

I have often heard it quoted:

Health is the wealth of the world!

I truly believe that to be true!

When you are young it is easy to feel invincible, and anything is possible.

This mindset is very positive and can be applauded; however there is no such thing as being invincible. It would be a foolhardy person that would think themselves invincible in all situations.

However, hold on to the thought that anything is possible, especially when choosing your ultimate goal!

Fill your mind with positivity! The sky is the limit!

Now that may seem an awful lot of hype, however, none of us know exactly how much we can do and if we put a limit on our goals we put a limit on our capabilities.

Someone quoted: "To see the limit of our possibilities we have to go beyond the possible!" (Was it Arthur C Clarke?)

To set your goals you must look at:

- - Your passion

- -Your skills

- -Your knowledge

- - Your "Toolbox" (all your life experiences, your skills, talents etc)

When you have self assessed and reviewed all the above you can then honestly say that your goal is in line with you and who you are.

What do you want to happen in five or 10 years?

Clearly visualize in the video, in your head, your appearance, where you want to live and what you want to have, in five years time.

Now imagine this goal is set on top of a block of flats - and to reach this goal you must climb many stairs with several steps on each stair.

To make it easier name each stairway as a year towards your goal.

If your goal is set for five years, then you will have five stairways.

Within each year you will have to perform each action that you have laid out towards reaching your goal in that year.

The best way to lay out your actions (for your goals) is to start on the stairway that is year four (if your goal is a five-year goal) and work your way back down to ground level that will be the present time (when you set your goal!).

If you doubt your abilities, or feel overwhelmed when thinking about long-term goals perhaps the best suggestion is to set a short-term goal.

As every action in life, it is best taken in small achievable steps. When you take achievable steps, they are always the best steps because they will build up your confidence and self-esteem thereby making you more motivated.

Having set a goal; It is important to write it down and immediately take action towards that goal.

It does not have to be a big action, but you have to take some action to set your brain in gear towards achieving the goal.

You may have failures along the way, as most people have but just hold your head up and carry on; failure is only a stepping stone to success. Next time you will succeed and success breeds success.

You may be completely satisfied with your situation in life; you may be quite happy with your family, your home, your surroundings, and that is quite okay.

However do not become complacent because it is always best to move forward.

Compare "life" with riding a bicycle - when you are sitting on a bicycle it is very hard to keep a balance unless you move forward. Life is very much like this, if you do not go forward, you will fall off.

Also letting your mind stagnate is not good, however-happy you are. It is in our genes to always move forward and to grow in knowledge and experiences.

Curiosity and necessity are two of the great catalyst that advanced the human race.

The necessity to survive, to eat and to procreate our species has enabled us to advance in the world.

It is an advantage for you to set achievable and realistic goals to start off with, and as you gain speed in your achievement your confidence and self esteem will be boosted.

Always lay out your goal in small little steps and as you obtain each step you will gain confidence. When you have your goals laid out you can review them and assess what skills and knowledge and what resources, you will need to go forward.

Start with the most manageable action towards your goals, and progress towards more challenging activities.

Many people who are not familiar with computers view them with fear and apprehension, hesitating even to switch them on in case they do some harm.

With the confidence to switch on, they will discover that nothing drastic will happen and gradually gain confidence to operate a computer.

It is the same in striving for your goal; small steps will get you there.

When you start out towards your goals, you can practice the habit of doing one small step each day towards that goal, it will quickly become a habit with you and quite soon you will be compelled to go towards, your goals with a feeling of excitement.

To gain your goals, you will need to exercise discipline, persistence and self-control.

Here are some steps towards gaining self control.

Your first action will be to set your goals and take immediate action on them. Take manageable steps given your capabilities and skills.

Put the first steps you need to take for your goals in writing and review each step, taking action with commitment and determination.

In the beginning, concentration is hard but as you find yourself succeeding with the little steps, you will start to gain confidence and have a feeling of pride.

You will become aware of your capabilities and determination, something you did not realize you had. Take control, take responsibility, and get a great feeling of self worth!

When you daydream, you will become more and more motivated towards achieving your dreams.

Run the video in your mind of your future as you want it and the more you dream of your future, the more inspired you will become.

Your will find it impossible to have a negative mindset anymore when you continually run the video of your success every day!

Every time you feel a little stressed or worried, run the video of the new future that you have planned in your goals and look at it with joy in your heart, imagining you are already there and enjoying your well earned success.

As you move towards your goals, celebrate each successful step and reward yourself in some way. After all you are doing all this for you, and you are worth it!

You have set this plan in place for yourself, and you deserve the credit and esteem for the courage to take responsibility for your future.

Trust in yourself - you are more than you think you are - you are unique!

If you are stuck in a job you detest you seriously need to review your situation in life.

If your financial situation stands the pressure, you will benefit by seeking a job that you know will be in line with your passion.

If you are not definite about your passion, review your life so far and identify the highlights, the times when you felt alive and motivated in what you are doing.

Whatever you were doing at these times was obviously something that ignited your passion then and will do so in the future. Moreover that is what you should be chasing now!

Whenever possibilities and opportunities present themselves to follow your passion you should be open to embracing them and to enhance your life.

Leaving your comfort zone may be necessary in order to make a big effort both in facing your fears and having to work a little bit extra to achieve a lot of success.

When you start following your heart's desire life becomes completely different, and you will feel enormous benefit in happiness and health.

People who are not following the passion in their jobs or career may find themselves suffering from bad sleeping habits, experiencing stress and being bemused and bewildered about where they are going in life.

Unless you are doing something that is in line with your interests in life, your passion, and sits comfortably with your principles and values you will not feel fulfilled or have a sense of high self-esteem.

If you are doing a monotonous, repetitive and uninteresting job every day then you will have no job satisfaction, leaving you feeling worthless and degraded.

The sure way to feel full of confidence and high self-esteem is to have a career that is rewarding and makes you feel you are making a difference to society.

You will notice that people, who work in rewarding professions, are self-assured and happy.

You can rest assured that they are eagerly looking forward to rewarding and fulfilling days at work!

Most people give eight hours of their life to the work environment each day(if you are lucky to have full-time employment) so it is extremely important to be relaxed and content working on something that gives you a morale boost each day.

When you follow where your heart leads you, where your passion is then you can be truly on your way to success.

Reality

1.   -What is your present fiscal, physical and mental situation?

2.   -What obstacles do you face?

3.   - What options have you got?

4.   - What resources do you possess (include your personal skills and strengths)? Check your "Toolbox"

Mission Statement

Before reviewing your reality, it is worth writing a "Mission Statement"

A mission statement will declare what you want to achieve during your life and will have been thought up with your principals and values being the guiding factors for your choices.

Life Chart

Below is a helpful chart to identify an area in your life that needs improving!

Tick the number that represents the state you are at, in each area of your life- 1 being low and 10 being high

Areas of your life	Low (Negative) (Positive)								High
Home									
Finance									
Social life									
Partner									
Dreams/Goals									
Spiritual									
Work/ life Balance									
Health									

The areas ticked on the left of the chart require looking into and if, below seven needs serious thought on setting goals for improvement.

Below are some questions to answer before completing the chart:

Home:

1   - Am I happy in my home?

2. - If not why?

3.   -What can I do about this?

4. - What will it cost?

5. - Am I financially secure?

6. - Emotionally?

7. - Who will it affect?

8. - Is it viable/feasible?

9. - What goals do I need to set to achieve the outcome I desire?

10. - Are there barriers to achieving those goals?

11. - What are the barriers?

12. - What are the ways that I can overcome the barriers?

13. - What else can I do?

14. - How will I feel when I achieve those goals?

Finance:-

Social Life:-

Partner:-

Dreams:-

Spiritual:-

Work/Life Balance:-

Health:-

The above questions should be asked about all areas of your life and the answers considered carefully before ticking the chart above.

This is a methodical and informed way to choose a topic for mini goal setting.

For major goals - Identify your passion.

Everyone has a particular passion, hobby or sport from which they experience a thrill..

Your goals should be connected in some positive way to your passion, thereby making it easier to stay focused and keep forging ahead towards your targets.

They should be in line with your talents and skills to ensure you are capable of achieving the most of what you set yourself to do without looking for outside help.

Work out what the rewards and benefits are from achieving your goals and who besides yourself will benefit.

Sometimes it is very motivating to know that someone that you love will gain from your efforts.

Ask yourself "Why"?
Why are you choosing this particular goal? Find at least three very strong reasons "why"

Will the achievement of this goal affect somebody in your life?
Will the achievement of this goal have a life changing effect on you?
Will this goal help you recover something from your past?

What exactly do you want from life?

If your best friend was giving a eulogy at your funeral, what would you like him/her to be able to say about you and your life's achievements? (Think seriously about it)!

How will you realize that you have reached your goal?

Imagine that you have reached your chosen goal!

See it in brilliant colour!

Hear the sounds surrounding you!

Feel the emotions of pleasure and satisfaction that reaching your goal will give you!

Smell the aroma on the breeze!

Be there completely!

What does it look like?

What are you doing?

What do you feel?

What are you wearing?

Where are you?

Who is with you?

What extra things are you able to do, that you have always wanted to do?

Who is enjoying your moment of glory?

Did you do it all yourself?

How did you know that it was possible?

What day is it?

What year is it?

Write out your goal in one sentence – make it SMART:-

S - Specific

M - Measurable

A - Achievable

R - Realistic

T - Timed

When you write your goals you are making a commitment, not just in your mind, but also in a physical form. It will be staring you in the face and scratching at your conscious until you reach the goal you have set.

When you write your goals, put them up somewhere where you see them every day. Put some photos that represent the goals alongside them – it may be a house you dream off or a car or yacht – do not put any ceiling on your imagination!

Just imagine all the wonderful things human beings have achieved even in the last 2 to 3 centuries.

It is amazing what has happened in the world progress-wise even within the last 50 years -just think about!

If you aim for the clouds – you will at least hit a high mountain!

Barriers

You will hit many barriers on your way to achieving your goals: this is a fact, as life is never that straight forward. The secret is to go around the barrier, not turn back and start again.

When you set out to somewhere that you have never been, and you take a wrong turning, you would not return home and start again would you?

If you use a SatNav you will be aware that if you go off the route, it will readjust and guide you from your present location to your destination.

Take a lesson from the SatNav, there is always a different way to get there.

There are always ways to foresee the barriers that you will encounter and plan around them.

Questions to ask about your goals:

What will I need?

Who can help me?

What may stop me?

Can I overcome that?

Whom will my goals affect? How will I get around that?

What else?

Now go and write your goals!

Ask yourself all the questions in this part of the course.

When you are 100% sure that those are the goals you want (having first studied your mission statement) post them up where you can see them and take a small step forward towards them every day.

Remember the Chinese Proverb:

"A journey of a thousand miles starts with a single step"

Having discipline and self control will speed you towards your goals!

Take these five steps to increase your self-control!

Your self control can be mastered one step at a time in the same way that you build your self-confidence and self-esteem. You have to gain trust in yourself and confidence that you can handle any situation, maintaining calmness and your ability to function no matter what problems or challenges are thrown at you.

Step 1

When your goals are clearly defined and you are clear in your mind of the reasons for your choice of goals, the "why" behind your choice, you are convinced that your choice of goals is in line with your passions; only then will you be focused on your targets.

When you look at your current reality, decide what needs to be addressed and strengthened in your life, such as your health, how healthily you eat, and if you smoke your willingness to stop this health-inhibiting habit and increase your exercise level.

If you are reluctant to take exercise, recruit some of your friends to join you on walks during the week.

Step 2

I am sure when you set out on a journey to a new destination you will get the roadmap out and plot your course.

The path to your goals is similar to roadmap and once you have written out your plan on how to reach your goals you will find yourself more motivated and focused.

As you progress on your plan you can tick off each item one by one and this will make you more and more motivated and more confident about your abilities to achieve your dreams.

Step 3

It is most important that once you set your goal plan, you go into action right away.

Choose one small step that you can take immediately and take that step forward; this will set you up with the right mindset to believe in yourself and to believe in your goal as you successfully take a small step forward.

You will find yourself truly committed and full of enthusiasm as you achieve your first step towards the life you have planned.

If one of your steps is to break a disempowering habit and you find it quite difficult, then break it down into

91

small steps, perhaps instead of expecting to achieve freedom from this habit immediately try spacing it over a week or perhaps longer.

Step 4

Your motivation will be fuelled by your daydreams and each successful step will help you to discover that your daydreams can become reality.

Visualize achieving your set goal with all the associated feelings, euphoria and enjoyment.

Play the video in your mind of where you are, what you are doing, what your surroundings are, if the sun is shining, if you can smell the flowers, what you are doing and with whom.

The "who you are with" can be very important if, for instance, your goal has been to stop smoking and one of your problems with smoking has been you bad breath - this will emphasize the "why" of your goal.

The "why" of your goal is the reason you will have set your goal and the stronger your "why" is, the greater your success will be.

Those facts will maintain your positivity and ensure you are not tempted by negativity.

If you ever find yourself veering towards negativity and doubting yourself stop and steer your mind towards a time in the past when you achieved a successful outcome and call to mind how you felt.

Again run the video in your mind and blow it up as big as you can and as bright as you can; doing this will help you to feel energized and confident to go forward with your project.

Step 5

When you make realistic choices when setting your goals, they become much more achievable and life so much more enhanced.

I will emphasize that one of the greatest incentives and motivation towards your goals is to choose the right "why" for your choice of goal!

When you become successful with your first small steps you will discover that life is not so bad after all and that achievement gives you a great feeling of self-esteem. You know you can do it!

Feel proud of yourself and acknowledge that you have the courage, the motivation, the persistence and the stamina necessary to become the person you dream of being.

To boost your self-confidence and self-esteem; give yourself a treat! Go on, celebrate. You know you are worth it.

*Dave Dineen first encountered sexual abuse at the age of seven. Through a stormy childhood he found himself placed in the care of a religious institution in Cork. His healing journey has been about learning to live with a difficult past. He is the CEO and **Founder of LÁMH Healing Foundation in Cork, Ireland.***

From the age of seven, all I can remember is being abused by my mother - physically as well as emotionally. She was horrendous in her abuse and had no problem tearing up the stair rods to beat me with. At bath time she'd push my head under the water. But I was a fighter and I'd challenge her. My father was a bystander. He didn't have a voice. He'd suffered from abuse in his own life, so in a sense it was normal to him. In the end my mother left him. My brother, Mick, also physically, and sexually, abused me. At night we'd share a bed, and the abuse continued. So night time was as terrifying as day. One day my brother beat me so hard I had to go to hospital. I went four or five times until eventually I told them what was going on and at the age of 12 was put in an adult mental institution. If I thought the abuse was going to stop there I was wrong. In those days people were allowed to roam free and do what they wanted. Later on I was moved to a Catholic residential school where one of Ireland's worst paedophile's resided. He was rampant. This was a special school where society put children they didn't want to see. My sense of shame flooded back.

The only person I confided in was my grandmother. So when eventually I was signed out of school at the age of 15, I thought it was because she'd been making a fuss, but years later I discovered it was my father.

As an escape I became heavily involved in drink and drugs and had my first child at 20. This was a key moment. Now I wasn't just a drug dealer, I was a father, and I wanted to make sure that my son didn't have the childhood I'd had. But it was hard to come off the drugs. Drugs suppressed the darkness I felt. And I looked at my son and thought, I don't know how to be kind, or caring or how to love.

As I reached the age of 30, along the way I set up business and slowly backed out of crime. I had three children by now and I was adamant I'd be a good father, put food on the table and *give them a clean house.*

Then one day I received a letter from Islington Social Services in London looking for a member of the Dineen family. I went over immediately and learnt how my brother and his wife were heroin/crack addicts, and they had six children now in care. Two of these children had been spotted climbing out of the window of a flat where they had been left as collateral for a drug debt. . As I listened to the story all the hurt and anger of my childhood came rushing back. So I set about looking for my brother - I intended to kill him.

In London I made several visits to see the kids but I'd also look in every hostel and crack house. Six months later I brought the kids to Ireland but it was a year before I found my brother.

One day I came out of Camden tube station, walked down the side road and saw a woman sitting on the step whose face was very familiar to me - it was my brother's wife. She looked gaunt and blue. Recognising her, I just screamed, "WHERE'S MICK?!

TELL ME WHERE HE IS!" She got such a fright, she couldn't answer, she could just point. In fact I'd walked right past him. He was a little further up the street, begging. Seeing my face, Mick's head dropped and his hands fell to his side. I ran towards him, searching in my pockets and looking around for something to kill him with, but, as I reached him my rage subsided and I just put my two arms around him and brought him to close to my chest, whispering in his ear... "Mick, I forgive you." And then I let him go. I had no idea I'd react like that. But in my heart I was given a choice. There were two ways of looking at the situation, one would lead to despair and darkness and the other to light and peace of mind. I took the road of light. It was an instant decision, a moment of opportunity and grace.

I saw Mick one last time after that. He came back to Ireland to see his children, but later died of a heroin overdose in Ireland. People can be freed from abuse. The media cover it by using stories of darkness and compensation, but I've always believed there is a way out of the darkness. I've been down so deep in the darkness - the pain, rage, self-medication and addiction - that I know there is a way out. For me forgiveness is like an escalator into the light. I took that chance and opportunity. I dislike the term "victims" because it places a weight on people. We aren't victims but human-beings who have been abused. By choosing forgiveness we can heal and let go and maximise our potential.

The above story has been republished by kind permission of the "Forgiveness Project" www.theforgivenessproject.com

Seven questions to help you sort your life!
1. What's crucial to resolve in your life right now?
2. How is that impacting your life?
3. What do you know you've been doing that is preventing you from resolving this?
4. What has this cost you in the past?
5. How is this affecting you now?
6. What's going to happen in the future if you don't get this resolved/achieved?
7. What decision are you making inside yourself right now?

Abuse help coaching-
http://www.TomMcAbuseRecoveryCoach.co.uk

http://tinyurl.com/j34asab (TomMc ARC)

Chapter 3

Reflections - What have you done about your pain and how have your actions affected you?

When I have a physical pain or an ache for any longer than a day or two I will go to a chemist and buy some painkillers!

That is normal.

However what happens when someone has an emotional pain, a pain that never seems to subside?

Many people may turn to drugs and alcohol to relieve their emotional pain and anguish.

Unfortunately drugs and alcohol work only as a temporary relief, they are not a cure!

In all cases they become a bigger problem than the pain that they were purported to alleviate.

Just about everyone focuses on what they do not want to have happen and invariably that is exactly what happens.

When you focus on the pain and the fact that you do not want the "pain" - you get more "pain".

Focus on good health and happiness and that is what you will get.

If your mind is focused on the fact that you do not "want to be poor" you will be "poor"

If you keep repeating "I am rich" your subconscious will keep striving to make you rich and you will find ways either big or small to move towards becoming richer.

Do not ever say I do not want, say I want!

Do not say I can't, say I can!

Your language can have a big impact on your state in life, therefore always make your language positive.

You life can be whatever you want it to be!

That may sound very airy fairy statement but it has been proven that if you focus your imagination on what you want and take steps towards achieving that, then it will happen.

Everything we have in this world has first been thought up in either our minds or someone else's mind before it became reality. When you set your thoughts on what you really long for and _not_ for what you want to avoid then you will be surprised how things can move in the right direction for you.

Do not ever let your thoughts be negative, instead of thinking I do not want this to happen, I don't want this disappointment, I do not want this rejection; think of the opposite, the positive and repeat it to yourself.

As you go through life many disappointments and sad things may happen to you but within each disappointment and challenge there is always a message of hope and strength if you look deeply for it.

Even within the greatest and most severe challenges in our lives when we look at them and figure out how we overcame them and survived through them, then we will begin to recognize our own strengths, our tenacity and in many cases, our courage.

This is a positive way of looking at your life, always seek something positive in everything that happens to you.

Every night before you go to bed review the day's events and pick out something positive and joyful.

It can be even something as trivial as the conversation with somebody that brightened up your day.

Always look for the positive.

When you have thoughts on the future always focus on the good things you want, not on what you want to avoid.

Believe in yourself and never doubt that you can achieve whatever you set your mind to, providing you believe you can!

Positive belief in yourself and visualizing a positive outcome from your efforts is the answer to achieving anything you want.

Visualize your desired outcome from whatever you set out to achieve and continue to envisage your goal several times a day for at least a month to manifest the result.

Many times in our life we encounter situations that we cannot control. It can seem that we will never escape from underneath the dark clouds, and we can be in a state of desperation not knowing what to do next. It is amazing how people can be happy and survive in those situations.

How do they get the fortitude, tenacity and stamina to carry on?

As the adage goes: "When the going gets tough the tough get going" however you may find this not all that easy to do!

When the "going gets tough" the following ideas on motivation will help!

Is motivation, a foundation stone of self-improvement?

There are many things that will encourage you to become motivated; for instance debt, losing out on our grades at school or college or even losing the opportunity of promotion at work or worse still getting dismissed from work because of not putting enough energy into your job.

Getting humiliated and embarrassed, shamed because we have not made the proper effort and have been shown up as lazy will certainly galvanize us towards up- rating our motivation.

A bad experience, a tragic story or a movie or book with an inspirational theme may kick- start us into becoming more motivated.

The following is a list of items in alphabetic order that can help you become more motivated.

A = Achieve your dreams. Do not associate with negative people, cultivate a circle of positive peers.

B = Believe in yourself, and your occupation. Believe that you are unique and important.

C-= Consider all problems from every direction and aspect.

D = do not give up. Do not give in. Remember how many times all the great inventors failed before they hit the jackpot. Keep going, success can be just round the corner.

E = Enjoy. Do not make money your reason for living, educate yourself as if you will live forever. Enjoy life and you will find that motivation comes easily.

F = Family and friends are important; do not take them for granted.

G = Give more than is needed. Put in extra effort and reap the rewards.

H = Hang on to your ambitions and dreams, as they will be your driving force.

I = Ignore those who criticize or try to pull you down. If criticism is constructive acknowledge it - if it is destructive ignore it.

J = Just be yourself and be true to yourself. The sure way to failure is trying to please everybody.

K = Keep trying even when things seem impossible. When you are motivated your problems will seem less daunting and your dreams will come easier.

L = Learn to love and respect yourself.

M = Make things happen, take action. When your dreams becomes actions they become reality.

N = Never tell lies or be dishonest, always be fair to everybody with whom you engage.

O = Open your eyes and your mind. Every coin has two sides, so always see both sides of every situation, problem or challenge.

P = Practice and become perfect. The more you practice the more skilled you become.

Q = Quitters never win, winners never quit. By being a winner you have to persist and go the extra mile.

R = Ready yourself and be always prepared. When you are motivated you will be ready and willing to go into action when opportunity calls.

S = Stop procrastinating. Just do it!

T = Take control of your destiny. Motivation is supported by self control and discipline and they are both important items in your self-growth.

U = Understand how others think, act and communicate. Always be prepared to listen and learn.

V = Visualize ahead of the event. Without vision you have nothing on which to use your motivation.

W = Want it more than life. When you dream you believe it is possible.

X - X Factor is what makes you unique. Your motivation is giving extra in everything you do, in every action you take towards others, your family, the care you give to your friends and the extra help you give to your workmates.

Y = You are unique and no one looks acts or talks like you. Cherish your life and the fact that you exist because life is not a rehearsal.

Z = Zest should be an integral part of your life. Excitement, enjoyment and interest are all parts of passion, and passion is the driving force behind motivation.

A positive attitude always helps, and if we believe in a Higher Power we can console ourselves that this is just a blip in our lives and will surely pass.

If you find yourself under a cloud and in deep trouble, I know it is no great consolation but everybody has a period of ill luck and it usually passes. The more upbeat you are in your outlook on life, the easier it will be to deal with this situation and the quicker it will improve.

There is an old saying in Ireland, if you had your troubles in one sack and somebody else's in another sack and you got a choice; you would choose your own sack. This is easily understood as we all know our own problems and how to deal with them much better than anyone else's problem.

We should find happiness and joy in even the smallest of pleasures in this life and not let little upsets destroy our sense of well-being and worthiness.

Can you do anything about your pain?
Burn Your Past!

Here is an exercise that will help:

Get a few sheets of paper to write on.

This next action may cause you some pain however it will be worth the effort.

Put your mind into a state of forgiveness.

Now the painful part, think back to your ordeal and write everything that comes into your mind concerning the event or events that caused you so much pain.

<u>Write everything; do not leave out any detail.</u>

When you have written every last horror, including your emotions and physical feelings at the time take them somewhere safe (like the kitchen sink) then

BURN THEM!!

Watch them burn with this thought in your mind:

That is the end of my torture – I have forgiven and my past abusers, tormentors and violators can no longer cause me pain!!

I am FREE!

Install a trigger – grip your right wrist with your left hand (or the opposite way, whatever feels most comfortable to you) as you perform the above exercise.

If you ever find yourself slipping towards your bad feelings again, repeat the trigger and you will remember the emotions you had when you did the "Burning Your Past" exercise!

Draw a deep, deep breath and let yourself feel good with a warm glow spreading through your body repeating:

That is the end of my torture – I have forgiven and my past abusers, tormentors and violators can no longer cause me pain!!

I am FREE!

I will now become happy and succeed in life!

Richard Levy was travelling in carriage number one on the Piccadilly Line on July 7th 2005 when Germaine Lindsay - a young convert to Islam blew himself up, killing himself and 26 passengers. Richard who lives in London and works in Marketing was badly burnt and received multiple injuries to his chest, side, feet and hearing.

It was the busiest train I can ever remember being on. In a strange way that saved people; I was protected from the full force of the blast by the people in front of me.

When I came round after the blast I realised that I was alive by the skin of my teeth. There was no carriage left, the sides and doors were all blown away and I'd been thrown against the electric cables of the tunnel. Soot was pouring down from the ceiling and there was a choking cloud of smoke. Instinctively I knew what had happened as there had been talk of a terrorist attack on the London Underground for months. It was no surprise to me.

Despite the utter carnage, I just knew I had to get out, because it was possible the whole place was going to go up in flames.

http://www.TomMcAbuseRecoveryCoach.co.uk

Then I saw a guy with a torch. He told me to climb out and pointed in the direction of Russell Square. I hobbled on to the rails and saw the driver standing there. At this point all I was looking for was someone in authority to tell me what to do. He was shouting at me because the blast had totally shattered my hearing, warning me not to touch the tracks because they may be live.

In hospital, my main concern was how many people had lost their lives alongside me. The experience bonds you and you want to honour the dead above all else. All you know is one minute you're on a train carriage with a whole bunch of people you've never met, and then bang the world changes. When I got out of hospital one of the first things I did was go to Kings Cross and lay some flowers in memory of those who didn't make it.

I feel it's desperately important to keep those people's memories alive. People remember the event but can all too easily forget that there were real people involved, and the devastating effect it can have on the people left behind.

At first my view about those who had done this to us was fairly ambivalent. The perpetrator was anyway dead so on whom could I vent my anger? I don't harbour blame toward anyone for what happened and banging on about British foreign policy is missing the point. There may well be a link but it's far more complicated than that. My only desire now is for understanding. I need to know why a 19-year-old would blow himself up in the name of a cause taking so many innocent people with him. If we don't understand we're in danger of history repeating itself. I don't believe in revenge but equally forgiveness doesn't seem like an adequate word. On the other hand understanding does; unless you understand how can you forgive? "The experience bonds you and you want to honour the dead above all else."

The above story has been republished by kind permission of the "Forgiveness Project" www.theforgivenessproject.com

Having read the story on the previous pages, I hope you are convinced to try forgiveness. Forgiveness is for you, not just for your violators. If you have not done the exercise at the beginning of this chapter, I urge you to do it now!

Seven questions to help you sort your life!

1. What's crucial to resolve in your life right now?
2. How is that impacting your life?
3. What do you know you've been doing that is preventing you from resolving this?
4. What has this cost you in the past?
5. How is this affecting you now?
6. What's going to happen in the future if you don't get this resolved/achieved?
7. What decision are you making inside yourself right now?

Abuse help coaching-
http://www.TomMcAbuseRecoveryCoach.co.uk

http://tinyurl.com/j34asab (TomMc ARC)

Chapter 4

Gravity - What are the seriousness and the consequences of abuse and violation experiences?

Drug and alcohol abuse are two of the most serious consequences to befall victims of abuse or bullying.

Addiction is a temporary emotional painkiller, from which the addiction grows into a bigger problem.

Taking risks

If you were lucky enough to take a holiday on the planes of Africa, you could watch the wildebeests as they weigh up the risk of having a drink.

These include the possibilities of either being eaten by lions or crocodiles or dying of thirst in the severe heat of the Serengeti.

More than 1 million wildebeests migrate from the Serengeti to the wetlands of the Masai Mara every summer.

Usually, the only water for this huge herd is the Grumeti River, which contains all the hazards of life and death for the herd.

They desperately need water to survive, yet the risk of death is ever present in the form of lions and crocodiles.

Only the very bravest, or the less aware, venture into the water to quench their thirst and, therefore, survive.

To the wildebeests, this is a life or death situation and is an unavoidable risk they have to take.

As we go through life, we humans will have risks to take but happily in most circumstances it will not involve a life or death decision.

In some cases, it may become a life and death decision as with addiction, which will ultimately become a slow death sentence.

To my mind, addiction is a slow form of suicide!

This may seem an extreme statement to most people, but when we seriously consider the health hazards of alcohol and drugs, it becomes obvious that they are a slow form of death.

To overcome either addiction, it is necessary to take risks and face our fears for the sake of long-term survival.

Let's consider the fears to be faced when deciding to free oneself from drugs or alcohol dependency.

Perhaps one of the biggest fears is the fear of stepping outside of your comfort zone and taking a risk on entering an unfamiliar lifestyle.

Despite the fact that addiction may lead to all manner of disasters, including perhaps homelessness and begging in order to support you and your habit, that lifestyle can become acceptable over time.

Once it becomes acceptable, then it becomes a comfort zone.

A comfort zone is a place where we all know what to expect and have a reasonable understanding of the outcome of our actions.

When we step outside of our comfort zone, we step into the unknown, which takes considerable courage.

Speaking of courage, I will state that fear does not equate to cowardice; it is simply not being aware of the full information and being misinformed of the risks.

False

Evidence

About

Reality

We may fear losing our identity.

Fear of losing who we consider to be our friends (other addicts), who may only consider us friends because we are an easy source to support their habits.

I have heard some people say that when they kicked their habit they felt a loss as if mourning a lost friend.

This ties in with the feeling of loss of identity because an addict can build up a label or title for themselves based on the addiction. When this label or title no longer exists, they are at a loss as to how they perceive themselves and how others perceive them now that they are free of their addiction.

Outside of the comfort zone there is also the fear of failure and the associated risks, such as criticism and "slagging" by their mates.

Can the fear of failure be overcome?

Fear of failure is a very common emotion.

It can be conquered and, for those who face fear head on, success is the reward.

If you let the fear of failure stop you, you are handicapping yourself from the very start. You will have to change your mindset and focus on winning whatever challenge you are facing.

You need a strong belief in yourself and completely banish all the self-doubt resulting from suppression in the past.

You will have to take criticism and ridicule from others as a sign of their jealousy of your success, not as something that is truthful or credible.

Set your mind on your achievements and successes, and look on your failures and mistakes as opportunities to learn and go forward with the knowledge gained from them.

Failure must be seen as a stepping stone to success.

If you build up failure in your mind and view it as embarrassing or humiliating, you will shy away from trying anything that leaves you open to failure.

Do not pay heed to negative thoughts about the possibility of failure. Become positive in your view of your abilities and build confidence in yourself. Review the evidence of the past and deep down you know you can succeed.

"I can and I will" should always be your motto!

Work up the courage to face this fear, give yourself the freedom to overcome it and go on to succeed.

The fear of failure may stop you in your tracks, resulting in procrastination. If you do not try, you will never know whether or not you are capable of success.

In fact, this fear is something you have manifested in your own mind and has no basis in reality, and prevents you from moving forward.

117

When exploring the consequences of failure, in regards to your ego, the possibility of a failure will have no value in the long term.

When you try to overcome this fear, you should look at your past successes and build your confidence to go forward, regardless of failure.

When looking at your past successes, review the actions and the factors that help you with those successes. When you experience success, you should reward your abilities, skills and persistence.

If you experience a "failure", do not blame yourself excessively; it is not normal for everyone to succeed at every attempt.

If you do have a failure, immediately review the way you approached the project or job, readjust your actions and try again. Change your methods and have another go.

Remember that if you give up without trying, your self-esteem and other people's perceptions of you will suffer as a result.

When you have a failure, take it as a learning experience and do not blame yourself; this will help prevent failure next time.

If you have a failure, ask yourself the following questions:-

At what stage did you make a mistake?

Could you have avoided making this mistake?

How can you upgrade your actions and improve?

Always understand the failure is a learning experience; that is, the more you learn, the more you know: the more you know, the more efficient you become.

Counseling/rehab is the pathway where professional support, encouragement and a disciplined environment is provided. I highly recommend anyone who needs help to avail themselves of it.

In counseling/rehab, you will receive continuous support to help overcome your fears.

I will make an observation here, which I hope will not feel out of place: I have met many people who have gone through rehab and returned to the companionship of their old friends who are still addicts.

Unfortunately, this is the worst situation due to the temptation to slip back into the addiction they have just overcome.

This is an unfortunate situation, especially for the homeless, as they have no option but to seek shelter wherever they can.

Unfortunately, as far as I am aware, there are no specialised shelters for recovered addicts; that is, safe places away from other active addicts.

Many homeless people, drug addicts and alcoholics are kind and supportive of their friends, despite the perceptions of the public.

I maintain that there is a streak of gold in every human being that shines through no matter what the personal circumstances. They are still able and willing to show compassion, love and support for their friends.

I have seen this demonstrated many times by my homeless friends.

Another fear is the fear of success and the responsibilities it can bring.

Dealing with success can present many problems for someone who has almost resigned themselves to having to struggle through life.

The answer is to convince yourself that you are worthy of success and definitely deserve it despite what people may have told you in the past.

Every human being was born to survive and thrive - everyone has success encoded in their DNA!

For inspiration have a look at this YouTube video-

<http://www.huffingtonpost.com/2011/11/08/quadruple-amputee-kyle-ma_n_1082059.html>

Your abusers, critics and anyone who has tried to put you down in the past are the real losers and you are the one who is really worthy and deserving of success.

In April 1999, three-year-old Isabel Maude suffered multiple organ failure and cardiac arrest as a result of doctors failing to recognise the life-threatening symptoms of Necrotising Fasciitis, a bacteria that rapidly eats the flesh. Isabel survived, but was left with a large wound requiring extensive plastic surgery.

Her parents, Charlotte and Jason Maude, decided not to sue the NHS over her treatment. Instead, working with the paediatric consultant who helped save Isabel's life, they have developed an online diagnosis tool to help doctors and nurses accurately diagnose illnesses in children. The system, developed by The Isabel Medical Charity, uses pattern recognition software to search for information in paediatric textbooks.

On day three of chicken pox Isabel developed a high fever and became very listless. We took her to our GP who said it was just a symptom of chicken pox. But that evening Isabel developed a purplish swelling around her tummy. This time we went to casualty where a very young doctor assured us was nothing to be alarmed about.

The next day she started vomiting blood. We

rang our GP who told us to ring A&E, but A&E just told us she was dehydrated. They thought we were just anxious parents panicking over our first experience of chicken pox.

In the end we were so desperate we walked into casualty with Isabel practically dead in our arms. Even then, when the nurse couldn't get a blood pressure reading, she blamed it on a broken instrument.

It was only when Isabel collapsed with delirium that people took notice. Immediately she was rushed away in an ambulance to St Mary's Paddington. That evening we were told she was displaying the potentially fatal symptoms of Toxic Shock Syndrome and Necrotising Fasciitis, also known as "the flesh-eating bug". It has a 60% mortality rate and the only way you can stop it is to cut away the infected flesh. In the surgery that followed Isabel had extensive areas of flesh around her tummy cut away.

We were in a state of shock, but you cope by dealing with each stage as it comes. On a couple of occasions we were told we would probably lose her, and if we didn't that she'd definitely be brain damaged. At one point she had a heart attack and they lost her pulse for half an hour. And then, miraculously, she started to recover. The doctors couldn't believe it. Once we knew she was going to live, a consultant intimated that we had been very badly treated by the other hospital. At the same time a lot of friends were urging us to sue; they said we could accumulate a pot of money in the bank for when Isabel was 18.

But it didn't feel right. We live in a blame culture where people now assume that if anything goes wrong you should sue. Yes, Isabel would have a rough time because of her surgery and subsequent deformity, but money wasn't going to help. By suing we would only have succeeded in putting doctors off medicine. It seemed somehow vindictive. We have forgiven the doctors for not spotting the potentially fatal symptoms. These newly qualified young doctors just don't have the experience to diagnose fatally sick children.

The doctors who have donated their time to help get Isabel up and running have all said the fact that we didn't sue the NHS made them sit up and think. To blame doctors for what had happened to our daughter would have achieved nothing. The creation of Isabel, on the other hand, could help to save children's lives. The beauty of Isabel is that it gives non-specialists the ability to become specialist consultants. We never dreamt it would become this big this fast. Some people have asked would we have sued if Isabel had died, and it's hard to know the answer to that one. But I don't think so. I hope not anyway.

The above story has been republished by kind permission of the "Forgiveness Project" www.theforgivenessproject.com

Abuse help coaching-
http://www.TomMcAbuseRecoveryCoach.co.uk

http://tinyurl.com/j34asab (TomMc ARC)

Chapter 5

Independence - What are your options for moving forward with your life?

Despite the drama and hurt encountered in your life, there is unquestionably a solid opportunity to rebuild your life and achieve your desired lifestyle.

By forgiving yourself and those who have traumatised and violated you; you reclaim the power you have been denied in the past.

To enable you to rebuild your life, I will outline the six emotional needs required to address the balance in your life.

When you study these emotional needs, you will become aware of the reasons why we act (react and respond) as we do in the many circumstances and situations that we find ourselves.

I lay out those needs to the acronym of "habits":

H - Humanity (compassion, love, understanding)

A - Altruism (giving, receiving, charity)

B - Belief (confidence, self belief, certainty, security)

126

I - Importance (self-esteem, significance)

T - Transition (growth, learning, going forward)

S - Selection (choice, options, variety)

Humanity - (compassion, love, understanding)

Humanity is the differentiating factor between the animal and human - if we did not have humanity we can very easily degenerate into a dog-eat-dog culture and end up in mayhem.

When the need for power and domination displaces our normal sense of humanity, we find that although we can succeed we will not ultimately win.

We have only to study world situations to confirm that statement.

"When the power of love overcomes the love of power the world will be at peace" (Unknown author believed to be Indian)

Humanity is compassion and consideration for others' needs.

Not just for others, but for our own needs and for the needs and feelings of all creatures on our planet.

Among certain sections of our community, it is regarded as being soft and in some cases being cowardly to have humanity.

When a youth can coldly kill another and brag about it, with the view to gaining standing and esteem among his peers and without the least show of consciousness or guilt - we need to seriously look at where the world is heading and where lack of humanity is taking us.

Without humanity, civilization will quickly end. Without humanity, we only think of the effect our actions will have on ourselves and we ignore the feelings or needs of others.

We are born with humanity - the ability to love and the need for love.

Love is what gives us our survival instincts and compels our parents to nurture us.

When we see a child firmly attached to a favourite toy or even a blanket, then we can see love at work; love and the need for love with which we as humans were born.

Having mentioned the horrific things humans are capable of doing, when we lose sight of our humanity, the question arises: what has happened in someone's life that causes them to degenerate to such a low level of civilization and commit heinous acts against fellow humans?

Have they been subjected to such a level of inhumanity and lack of love, compassion and respect that they think it is normal to act in a jungle fashion without any feelings of conscience?

As with everything else in life, when we show humanity - love and compassion it will be reflected back to us a thousand fold.

If there are any doubts about this, consider the question: what do you get from an enemy?

The answer?

Trouble and pain!

When you make friends you get all the benefits of friendship; help, support and a secure feeling that you are not alone.

Humanity is essential in all our relationships; we must be able to recognize and consider others needs - especially in a relationship or marriage.

The biggest causes of breakups are lack of understanding of the other person's needs and their point of view.

There are many times we have to look hard at causes of stress between our partners and work out what is missing in regards to their human emotional needs - most times it can be a feeling of not being loved or not being made feel important that is causing their doubts.

In a relationship the important thing to remember is to communicate and listen to each other with humanity and compassion.

When we talk about humanity, we are inclined to think about humility - which is taking humanity to its highest degree.

However to exercise our humanity we do not need to allow ourselves to become humiliated.

When a person becomes humiliated, it is usually from being bullied or embarrassed in some unjustifiable way.

Using our humanity in a healthy and normal way is just exercising our natural feeling of love, compassion, understanding, mercifulness and sympathy towards others, especially in times of their need.

The opposite to humanity is arrogance and that is a trait that never serves any good for anyone.

Most great heroes and heroines throughout the ages have shown strong humanity and great love for their fellow humans.

Florence Nightingale is a well-known example of compassion and care.

She was of course the founder of modern nursing care and culture - a culture that has saved millions of lives.

There are thousands, even millions of heroic examples of love and this is happening every day all over the world, frequently in war zones where brave soldiers put themselves in grave danger to either shield or rescue a comrade who is at risk.

"Love is the fruit of sacrifice; Wealth is the fruit of generosity" Quote from the 44th verse of the Tao. Change your thoughts change your life. Dr Wayne W Dyer.

Without humanity the human race would degenerate into chaos. We would lose all sense of right and wrong, become completely immoral and use the law of the jungle; survival of the fittest!

Throughout the years it has been proven that when a group of people or one individual chooses to live by the "law of the fittest" (the law of the jungle) and suppresses the rest of their countrymen, (in some cases taking over other countries) - it may work for a period of time but in the end justice and humanity will win.

We can take for example world War 11 or any leader who set themselves up to suppress their people who ultimately became a cropper when there was a rebellion.

The only sane way for the human race to survive is cooperation and use teamwork, with everybody using their humanity!

I described humanity as, love, compassion, mercy, kindness, sympathy etc - now we will discuss "love"

Love

Most people have several different ways of understanding love, and it is not easy to state exactly what love is.

A quote here from the Road Less Travelled by M Scott Peck on "love"

Love is "The will to extend oneself for the purpose of nurturing one's own or another's spiritual growth"

I would personally add "material growth" as well as spiritual.

The way I understand it is that when we love others we are concerned for their welfare both materially and spiritually.

First and foremost we must love ourselves because if we do not love and respect ourselves we cannot have the capacity to love anyone else.

The love we have for our partners, family and siblings will be more acute and fervent than the love we show for our other fellow humans.

Nevertheless when we show concern for the rest of humanity, we are shown a degree of love that we were all born with.

When we deny this love which is merely our natural human nature, we can easily let destructive emotions into our lives, emotions like jealousy and hatred.

When we feel low in confidence and self-esteem we can very easily become jealous and begrudging of our peers.

When the self-confidence is low it is hard to accept your work colleagues and your peers getting ahead while you are standing still.

Further on in this book, I will present ways to build self-confidence and self-esteem.

The same love is mostly viewed as making love; that is, having sex.

Now, I regard term making love in two different ways!

The first is where there is clear affection and a strong desire to make the partner happy; as in most marriages and partnerships.

The second is making love (having sex) purely for sexual gratification, regardless of the consequences to the welfare of the other person involved. For example, where one or both people involved are extremely intoxicated or in the case of "rape".

I cannot realistically see any true affection or care evident in those circumstances. It is just "lust" not love!

Remember the definition of love that I wrote to nurture one's own and others spiritual (I added material) growth!

The meaning of love that is commonly understood is a feeling of rapport, compassion and understanding that we, as humans, are capable of showing to each other.

This love is a catalyst for most of the good actions in the world - such as the help given to nations who are in need, as a result of famine or government mismanagement.

This thought leads to the fact that humanity is also to understand and tolerate all other humans of different cultures, race, religion, colour or whatever their differences from us may be.

We are all human and each one of us is unique in different ways. No two people are exactly alike; even identical twins. They may look similar, but their brains are different.

We may become prejudiced towards some cultures through what we read in the media. However, by doing this, we are "generalizing", which is dangerous.

Generalising, means to over simplify, to take a broad view. In other words, to take as true that which is reported about any culture is applicable to everyone from that culture.

Personally, I trust everyone unless they prove me wrong!

Now you may think all this humanity, love, compassion is fine, but will it leave you open to exploitation?

You will become more popular among your friends and, subsequently, you will gain more self-confidence and self-esteem.

However, you need not become so loving and kind that you let others take advantage. As a result of your new-found self-esteem, you become more aware that you are a person of worth and that others should treat you as such.

You do not necessarily have to lose your assertiveness to become a person of humanity!

No one could accuse Richard Branson or Bill Gates of being exploitable or an "easy pushover", yet they are both hugely invested in helping the less fortunate of the world.

They both give vast amounts of money for medical research and for resources of health and welfare in the African continent.

You do not have to become a victim or be perceived as an easy target when you exercise your humanity; in fact, you will be viewed as a noble person by your peers.

Being full of humanity and care means everyone will be willing to return your actions:

"We are all mirrors; what you project to others will be reflected back to you!" This statement is true.

I am sure you know many unfriendly and unhelpful people? How many would you go the extra mile for?

If you are a caring person, you may feel like helping those people when they are really in trouble, but you will be inclined to place a limit on your efforts.

However, if they were people who would rush to help you when in need, there will be no limits to your help.

People who have compassion and care for others are almost without exception held in high regard in their own community and will always receive support when in need.

I coach homeless people some of whom are alcoholic and others take drugs. The alcoholics are sometimes contrary and even abusive towards others; particularly, those who are helping them the most.

However, if they are caring and helpful when sober then they will be tolerated and afforded greater leniency than those who are normally morose and unfriendly in their sober state.

Some who are willing to help others and the staff in the "Shelter"; are truly cherished.

This bears out the "you are a mirror" statement.

I have seen the goodness and true humanity and care that is natural to most of this group of people and it always urges me to try and help them to sort their lives.

In most cases, each of them is more anxious to help their peers than they are to help themselves.

This neglect of self is where their humanity is weakest - they do not always love themselves.

Love and care should start with oneself, not in a selfish way, like always putting yourself first, but in a healthy way.

Do not neglect yourself or your family.

Our priorities should always be for our own welfare, followed by our family and the wider world.

Give and take

I have seen some people who always take and can never give. This is not the natural way of the world and they have many reasons.

Those people may have always got whatever they demanded when children or maybe they were denied their share of love or worldly goods when young and have decided to grab it all now.

For whatever reason, they are now selfish and will not give anything in return.

This does not enhance their reputation or earn any love or care from their peers and they then truly lose the goodwill of all but their close friends - sometimes they also lose the love of their families.

I have heard a story from a friend - I did not read this myself:

There is reported to be a breed of penguins in the Antarctic, who groom each other to get rid of pests that sucked their blood!

One of the penguins availed of his peers grooming and promptly waddled off without returning the favour; this happened for a few days until it dawned on his mates that he was not doing his share.

They promptly ignored him!

Guess what? -It is not a pleasant thought, but he was literally eaten alive!

So even in the natural world, humanity, caring for others and fair play rule supreme.

Give and take; playing fair and standing your place in your community are solid ethics that will serve you well!

Humanitarian heroes

We can call to mind some great examples of wonderful individuals, who give and give and seldom receive any material items in return.

There are thousands of missionaries, doctors, nurses and lay people who dedicate their lives to the benefit of others; they do not usually get great rewards but they have enormous satisfaction and emotional fulfillment in following their passions.

Almost all of them put their lives on the line, In most countries where their expertise is required, they are met with abuse and persecution.

Their dedication is the ultimate example of humanity!

Team players who are always willing to help and cooperate are held in the highest of respect in the communities and workplaces.

They are the ones on the promotion list in all companies and if you want to get on you have to practice the culture of humanity, tolerance and compassion; be willing to help and support your peers.

Willingness to tolerate and evaluate alternative perspectives is essential for the advancement in any business.

Altruism (giving, receiving, charity)

How do you feel about the advantages and disadvantages you face in life?

No matter how poor your current quality of life, be asured that someone somewhere is having a worse time.

We moan and groan; wallow in self-pity. But when we weigh up our advantages and good fortune, both in terms of health and material goods, we should be jumping for joy.

We live in a free country; not just freedom of speech and movement, but many of life's essentials are free for the taking!

When we consider the difference in quality of life in the UK and America compared with some countries that have an oppressive leadership, we may feel guilty for our good fortune.

We should not feel guilty of course, because our ancestors fought and died for our right to freedom.

A great way to embrace life is to share your blessings and help others enjoy their lives.

Altruism - charity and contribution are one and the same, and a wonderful way to enhance others' and our own lives.

When you help a charity work or contribute to a worthy cause, you will have a feeling of worth. Deep down you know that you have given "something back".

"You have to give before you get".

A simple way of being honest and realistic is to share your knowledge and skills for the benefit of others.

People with special skills can volunteer with charitable organizations to teach their skills and enhance the lives of the charities' clients.

It may be computer skills or maybe cooking expertise - whatever we know can be of great value to those who need our knowledge.

Getting involved with charities and volunteering, meeting more people, feeling more valued by becoming part of the community, earning prestige and getting the support of many good people in return for just a little effort.

When you are a supporting person, you will find that you are in a circle of like-minded people who support each other as well as the charity to which they subscribe.

I like to volunteer, as the work focuses directly on the client and the benefits are obvious and transparent.

There are thousands of charitable organizations who deal direct with their clients; such as homeless shelters, youth organizations and many others.

When you work with these charities, you see the results of your efforts and can get a great sense of satisfaction from seeing the way that you are improving someone's life.

Millions of people overvalue their money and their health for others; therefore, they refuse to give to or help anyone.

Money is only paper or coins; you cannot eat it. As long as we have enough to survive and a little over, we will be ok!

If you will always see yourself as needy, you will always be needy!

If you consider that you have enough and are willing to share; you will always have enough to get by and more.

"What you share doubles in value; both for you and for those you share with!"

My quotation!

There was a wonderful couple featured in the national papers who won a magnificent £48 million on the lottery; their first thoughts were how they could help their immediate families and close friends.

Their reasoning was that they could not enjoy it unless they shared it!

What a wonderful couple; long may they enjoy good fortune!

That is the way to live!

Instead of jealously guarding what we have, be it big or small, if we share it, it becomes infinitely more valuable.

The same applies to what we have not got. We should never be jealous or begrudging of others who appear to be better off than us.

I have seen many extremely rich people on TV and, amazingly, they have a worried look in their eyes; does wealth automatically guarantee happiness?

Sorry; it does not!

Contributing to a charity is a noble idea and however small our contribution is, it is just as important as the big-money that millionaires and billionaires give; percentage-wise we are giving more.

I strive to explain what I mean; when you give a few pounds to a good charity, you are probably giving a larger percentage of your wealth than say a millionaire or billionaire.

Some senior citizens donate a big percentage of their income to charity, which is undoubtedly a noble act.

Contributing to charity is not the only contribution of which we are all capable.

When we go to work and pay our taxes, we are contributing to the country as a whole.

We are also building our own feeling of self-worth.

If you are unemployed, you will have the extra problem of low self-esteem because you will lack the pride you would have if you had a job and were self-sufficient.

When you can provide the necessities of life for yourself and others, you will have high self-esteem and pride in yourself.

Millions of people are unemployed, mostly through no fault of their own I would never criticize those who are genuinely trying to get work; they are suffering both physically and emotionally.

Unfortunately, the longer an individual is unemployed, the easier it becomes to make unemployment your comfort zone; no worries, the "state" will provide.

This is a disastrous way of thinking, you lose your self-worth, and doubts about yourself and your future set in; a short step away from depression.

The best way to avoid this situation is to stay positive and focus on getting work, for however long it takes.

Volunteering is a good idea when you are unemployed and can be a pathway to a paid job. It is another form of altruism and will add to your feel-good state.

Do not sit around and watch television or drown your sorrows in the pub.

I know of one young lady who began to volunteer during a period of unemployment.

When she was volunteering part-time, the management offered her a full-time job.

Altruism is its own reward!

Belief (confidence, self belief, certainty, security)

Why do I feel insecure and self-conscious?

Why do I feel so upset when others disagree with me?

Security in life is when we feel confident and have strong self-belief.

When we were about 1 to 2 years old, we had no inhibitions and although we were not aware of our confidence we did not have much doubt; we expected to be looked after.

Then, when our thoughts that all we had to do was ask and our wishes were automatically granted, reality sets in and our parents, if they were responsible people realise that we had to learn boundaries and the difference between what was right and wrong.

Up to 1-years old, most babies have the world as their oyster - their wish is their parents' command.

Suddenly, the world changes; parents realize that every baby will need to do things for themselves (or at least they should realize it) and a new word enters the language - "no"

We start to become individuals and grow in our own particular way (we are all different).

We gain a little confidence with the security of our home and mum and dad - then we go to school!

Some will sail through school and college, while others will lose a lot of the little confidence they had gained.

As we grow up and go through our school years, we will be knocked by criticism from teachers, peers and sometimes be even bullied by others.

It is no surprise, therefore, that our confidence may slump as we approach adulthood.

Your confidence and self-belief is built on your life experiences - if you have been experiencing knock backs and hardships, you will have a battle to keep your confidence at a reasonable level.

Conversely, if life is good to you, it should be easier to maintain a normal level of confidence.

When confidence drops, we review each new task or situation with a certain amount of fear, then we need to find a way to build our self belief; become more assertive and self-reliant.

Even the most fearful of us has some situation or tasks in which we will feel very confident and relaxed.

This feeling of relaxed confidence is required to build on and the best way to do that is to recall your feelings as you performed those tasks or your feelings in the situation where you are confident.

Bring these emotions back to your mind and visualise them in full colour, the sounds you experienced and even the feeling of the air and the aroma around you; all with full emotion.

When you feel low in confidence, this is a great way to build yourself up again.

Imagine you are looking at your confident self in a video and make it in full colour.

This will build yourself belief as you will know that you are capable of confidence in certain situations and therefore can apply it to a new job or situation.

Very few people are completely confident when going for a job or business interview; a good way to prepare is to use visualization.

You will of course have prepared and thought of all the answers to the possible questions you may be asked.

You know what the outcome should be; perhaps the interviewer shaking your hand and saying; "you have been selected!"

Okay, hold that idea for a moment; imagine you are looking at yourself in a video and you have just finished your interview, now feel your interviewee shake your hand and hear him or her tell you what you want to hear - feel the joy, see it all in full colour!

Do this several times for a few days before your interview and you will gain confidence that success is yours.

You can do this for any situation that you face in life. Be positive; believe it and it will happen.

If your confidence and self-belief is really low, you can build it by recognizing your individuality and uniqueness.

You have a lifetime of experiences and skills to refer to and to be proud and confident about.

We all tend to be humble about our achievements but this does not help our confidence.

Write your experiences of life, your skills, your qualifications, your good characteristics - what you have done for others etc in a notebook and then stop and read it often. I call this your "Toolbox".

Your Toolbox is in fact a combination of your principles and values, and all your life experiences- write them all down!

This is you!

Be proud of yourself; you are unique!

There are no two people the same in this world; we are all unique.

This is the way to build self-belief!

When we build our lives emotionally, we will gain materially; thus becoming self-sufficient.

Being self-sufficient and looking after ourselves without reliance on others will boost our security, confidence and self-belief.

Not everyone looks to be able to provide for their needs, but if you cannot, at least the desire to do so is a step in the right direction.

Having the right positive attitude is essential for any achievement in life - if you think you can you will; if you think you cannot you won't.

It is simple; everything we do starts in our mind!

There are many ways in which our confidence and security and self belief can be weakened.

We may have heavy commitments like a big mortgage, family to support and educate; all those things make us fearful for our survival and in some cases make us vulnerable in our careers.

When financial demands become severe, we can lose confidence and be less assertive.

This leaves us open to abuse and exploitation in some respects.

Consider the case of a young man or woman with a family and mortgage. It may seem impossible to change jobs, simply because it takes a lot of courage and confidence in oneself to leave your comfort zone (a job you know) and take a chance on the unknown.

A situation like this involves much confidence building and realistic evaluation of the pros and cons.

Having a family to love and be loved by in a friendly home is a sure confidence booster; unfortunately, not everyone is that lucky and will have to build confidence in other ways.

Some people who are low in confidence become aggressive and often become bullies, just to boost their ego.

I have known people in my life was suffer from very low confidence and self-esteem and were covering it up by being arrogant, aggressive and very jealous minded.

People like this are usually very insecure and always trying to blame others for their mistakes; spending their time covering up for their shortcomings.

In my life, I have never claimed to be faultless or infallible.

I have found that if I ever made a mistake, the best course of action is to own up immediately and try and sort it out.

There was a maxim in my youth; "The truth can be blamed but it can never be shamed!"

This is an indisputable fact!

When you own up to a mistake, people will see you as honest and deserving of their trust.

To succeed in life you need people to know you, like you and trust you; being honest is the only way to have people "trust you".

Examples of strong confidence and self-belief were demonstrated to brilliant effect at the London 2012 Olympics; all the medal winners displayed extreme confidence, such as Usian Bolt and Mo Farrah.

I have no doubt that both could see themselves crossing the line in first place even before the race began.

I have no proof but I guess they visualized this many times before the contest.

This is the power of visualization!

Honesty is a hallmark of a confident person, a person with belief in themselves, just as lying and being deceitful is a sure sign of low confidence and low self-esteem.

Honesty builds self confidence as you know that when you are being honest you cannot be caught out or shamed. You will gain confidence, belief and pride in yourself.

Frequently, many may feel threatened or slightly bullied, and that is not a good feeling.

First of all let's look at the mindset of a bully; a bully is usually someone who feels inferior themselves and is trying to boost their ego by putting someone "down".

Bullies are control freaks who only feel confident and good about themselves when they feel that they are in control of others and all situations that may affect them.

When they cannot control the situation that they find themselves in - or the people they are interacting with, they feel vulnerable and frightened.

This is the last thing they will want you to know and will try their best to cover up their insecurities by picking on someone less physically fit or confident than themselves.

Bullies are lacking in confidence and continually need to have their ego boosted by seeing others submit to their wishes.

Putting it bluntly bullies are cowards!

When they are resisted, they will back down and show that they are really the frightened ones.

When a bully who is a control freak is ignored and does not get the attention and reaction from the one they are abusing – they become really frustrated and will try all sorts of devious actions to achieve their aims.

They will tell lies and twist the truth of any situation in their efforts to malign and discredit the one they are abusing.

Now bullies think they are "looking down on you" - it is important to remember that for someone to look down on you "you have to lie down first".

In other words, if you can realistically stand up to a bully, they will back down and leave you alone.

Zapping your self- belief by verbal attack

I have had one or two people (through the course of my life) verbally attack me. Luckily, I was able to stand and listen without letting it affect me adversely.

After about 2 to 3 minutes, when the verbal attacker had to stop to gain their breadth, I said with a smile "go on keep going, I was just getting interested!"

I found that they walked away in frustration!

If you want to try that approach; please ensure there is no possible way that your attacker will resort to physical violence.

Moreover, be confident enough to take the verbal abuse without it affecting you emotionally, otherwise just try and walk away.

"No one can hurt you unless you allow them" Eleanor Roosevelt.

She was of course talking about verbal or emotional hurt.

If you see that you may be exposed to a violent situation or are living in a violent neighborhood, it may be a wise precaution to have some self-defense training.

Most self-defense disciplines are solely for protection, rather than for use in aggression.

Being proficient in a self-defense discipline is a great morale and confidence booster.

If your physical condition is not up to standard, your confidence and self-belief will likewise be lacking.

You will need to get out and get fit.

Before you do, please consult your doctor to ensure you are able to take exercise.

I believe in walking, as it is the less impactful exercise one can take; walking has no impact on the joints like jogging.

However, whatever type of exercise is your favourite is best.

When walking or jogging you do not spend money by joining a gym and you will benefit from the open air and the scenic views. Being fit will support your confidence and self-belief and will help you become progressively more self-assured.

Having self-belief and self-confidence is all in the mind and you can build them by acknowledging your own powers, skills and talents.

We spend far too much time worrying about what others think of us; how they view us as regards our looks, our capabilities and our characters.

Ultimately, it does not matter what others think, it is what we think ourselves that matters.

What others think cannot realistically harm us unless we let it.

If you are easily upset by people's comments, however well-meaning, a good game to play is hiding behind the invisible curtain.

Pretend there is an invisible curtain between yourself and whoever is commenting on you and they cannot touch you either physically or verbally.

Pull the curtain in your mind and blank out the feeling.

When we think of appearing in a vulnerable situation - for instance on a stage in a play or doing a presentation - we usually have unrealistic thoughts about how people view us; we worry about how we sound, how we look and everything in between.

In reality, if we are sincere and honest about what we are doing, everyone will think we are wonderful.

Even if they do not, does it matter - we will live!

It is not a life or death situation.

The same goes for all situations when your self-consciousness and shyness can appear; it really does not matter all that much so long as we are honest and sincere in what we do, we will be accepted and in most cases applauded for our efforts.

Shyness can be a debilitating problem and can stop us achieving our true potential in many instances.

If you suffer from shyness, try looking at yourself in the mirror and saying "I am not embarrassed". Repeat this every day and watch for changes. It takes persistence to overcome shyness for anyone who is easily embarrassed, so keep at it every day.

The surest way to change anything in your life is one small step at a time.

Almost everything in life can be changed by small steps, taken consistently.

Here are some ways to consolidate your self-confidence and certainty.

1

Identify an action or situation that you are confident at and build on that by visualization. Run the video in your mind.

2

Make a list of your achievements, experiences, principles, values and skills; your life in fact and credit yourself for the unique person that you are.

3

Always think positive.

4

Visualize yourself winning/achieving your desired outcome every time before the event.

5

Remember that no one can make you feel inferior unless you let them.

6

Whatever you do in life, if it is your honest and sincerest best, you will succeed.

7 Confidence and self-belief are in your mind; only you can process it and not let anyone take it from you.

Importance (self-esteem, significance)

Why do I always think I am being overlooked and underappreciated?

When you practice humanity and gain confidence and self-belief through altruism, esteem, importance, significance will almost come to you automatically!

Lack of self-esteem is when we find ourselves comparing with others and trying to gain popularity in any way possible.

We try to boost our ego.

In our present-day society it has become the norm to show off in the most outlandish way just to gain "celebrity" status.

It seems that morals, principles and values are cast aside in the race for notoriety - even among our ruling classes!

This type of notoriety or celebrity does not achieve lasting esteem or a feeling of true self-worth.

Notoriety and celebrity do not result in gaining respect and respect is the only true measure of self esteem.

The only true way to gain respect is to give it to everyone you encounter and communicate with in any way.

I say communicate with because, if you do not tell the truth and be honest, you are not being respectful.

Anyone who tells you a lie is belittling you in the most severe way.

When someone tells you a lie they are not only trying to deceive you, they are telling you that they think you are stupid and naive, because that is what they believe when they think you will believe an obvious lie.

Think about it!

Is that not what you think when you tell someone a lie?

Being respectful

Being respectful is really easy for us when we gain confidence enough to be able to think "I am equal to everyone else and they are equal to me".

"I don't have to prove I am superior and I don't have to make them inferior to make myself feel important!"

"I am my own man/woman and I know that I am unique - there is no one exactly like me and I am happy with who I am!"

When you get into the habit of hesitating for a mini second before you speak and figure out whether what you are about to say is going to please or displease your audience, then you are showing respect to everyone.

Is it going to improve their day?

Is it going to improve their image of you?

Will it improve their image of themselves?

Is it going to improve their image of people you talk about?

167

- If it is not; be aware that you are pulling down the people that you talk about and you are lowering your own self-image as well, nobody admires a slanderer.

"What you do to others; you do to yourself!"

Self-respect - living to a code of conduct that shows your credibility and displays your values is part of being respectful; being aware of your language, no swearing and no aggressiveness in your attitude.

A quick word on swearing:

Swearing is usually picked up from one's peers and can become an unconscious habit. It is quite ugly and can be seen by many as insulting and abusive.

It is against the law and regarded as assault by police. Indeed, you can be arrested for swearing, especially if you are intoxicated.

Swearing may be tolerated in certain situations (eg. on a building site), but certainly not in public if you wish to gain respect.

Swearing also demonstrates a lack of knowledge of the English language (or if you swear in any other dialect). When you have to use swear words to emphasize your point, you are highlighting that you do not know the proper adjectives to use.

Wealth

Wealth is not a sign of respect or high self-esteem; it will afford you a certain feeling of security and is very satisfying. However, although it is no guarantee of happiness or contentment, it is definitely preferable to being poor.

You will feel some self-respect when earning a good honest living and are self-sufficient.

I know a few people who are only moderately rich and are extremely well respected; mostly because of their honesty, integrity and their acts of helpfulness towards their less well-off peers.

When you use the principle of honesty/truthfulness, and humanity/tolerance in your life, you will automatically earn high self-esteem and significance in your community.

I know some people who are honest and truthful but at the same time lack humanity and will bluntly state their opinion of someone or some situation without regard to humanity (consider others have feelings) and they wonder why they are not held in high regard in their community.

It is okay to be honest with your opinion; but you need to use decorum and sensitivity towards others' feelings.

You need to practice all principles above (honesty/truthfulness, humanity/tolerance) to gain high respect from those in your life.

A popular view among the youth at present is that you have to become a "celebrity" to gain respect but being a celebrity does not automatically earn you respect; it may get you some money, sometimes in the short term (when others are earning money from your talents) but it can be very short-lived.

One minute you can be at the top and the next you are dumped and never heard of again.

Celebrity status can be great; if you have a great talent like singing, musician or sport skills set, by all means go for it. Just keep your feet on the ground!

Do not get carried away by your new-found fame; remember you are human and subject to the same rules as the rest of us; the rules of our emotional states.

We are all subject to our emotional needs and, unless we are balanced, we lose our way in life.

Some celebrity's think that they are so popular, they can cheat, lie and behave outrageously and not reap any consequences.

This is when it all crashes!

You can include our governing classes, our MPs etc in that category.

When the principals of honesty/truthfulness, humanity/tolerance are ignored all respect, self-esteem and significance is forfeited.

To gain importance, respect, esteem and significance from all your acquaintances, it is essential to first of all respect others and yourself by maintaining high standards of conduct.

If you find yourself being aggressive and ill mannered towards others, you need to look inwards, rather than at the recipients of your abuse.

The person you are disrespecting may well be unworthy of respect but nevertheless when you disrespect them, you lower your standards of conduct and your own self-worth.

By all means be assertive in your dealings with the public at large, but always be aware of the fine line between aggression and assertiveness.

To be assertive without aggression you need practice and strong self-confidence.

Transition (growth, learning, going forward, improvement)

Why do I feel left out and unable to join in?

Have you achieved at school or did you just not bother?

Was it all just not worth the effort?

There are millions of people who regret not making enough of an effort at school and now feel left behind.

Thankfully, we live in a world where nobody should feel left behind educationally; there are so many opportunities for adult learning, we need never stop improving our lives.

You can (and should) set a goal of learning at least one new skill each year!

Even if you are a senior citizen you should keep your mind active and learn something new each year. It is a great way to pass the time when you are retired.

You may wonder what you should learn about, what would interest you most.

Have you got a hobby or interest in any subject? If you can find a subject that you could feel passionate about - that is the one to go for.

Whatever ignites your passion, will change your life in an unbelievable way when you can follow your passion in your career or whatever projects you undertake.

I would say that if you are not passionate about your job, you will never climb the ladder of success. If you are passionate about your job you will learn everything possible to help you and, therefore, you must advance.

As babies have to learn to talk, the next great skill we learn is to read. Reading is the window to the world and a positive box to our brains. Your brain is your bank (and your bank manager).

Whatever knowledge you put in your brain is building your "Life Bank" account and will be there for your use when you want it.

There is no way you cannot learn something new every day unless you are completely unaware of what is going on around you.

We learn from the actions of others, the actions of nature and from our own response to life situations. It is a continuous learning process if only we observe life properly.

We should look for information about everything, you never know what little bit of knowledge will turn out to be the catalyst to your future.

We need to learn how to control our lives; materially, spiritually and financially.

That is a lot of information to acquire.

When we consider how much useless stuff we read and still have room to store daily essential information, the capacity of our brain is amazing.

One item that most be of the population never learned is the subject and control of their spending.

If you have a wage or salary of £30,000 per year and you are spending is 30,500 you are worse of than if you were jobless!

If you are spending £29,000 then you are rich! (simple arithmetic!).

Forget about living on credit - it does not work in a shrinking economy.

It never really worked, even in inflation.

You should never rely on credit (except perhaps for a mortgage), regardless of the state of the economy.

There is a popular rule of thumb that everybody should save at least 10% of their income. I highly recommend that advice!

To be successful, indeed to comfortably survive, you will need to continually learn new information every day.

If we ask ourselves each night, "did I learn something today?" and be able to truthfully say "yes" and ponder on the lesson of the day, we can be assured we are improving each day.

The first function of our brain when we were born was to learn - and for our natural survival we shall continue to learn until we switch off.

Do you ever wonder how the world keeps advancing and every day thousands, possibly millions, of new inventions are thought up.

New inventions are not usually a completely new idea; in fact most inventions are a combination of several different ideas.

So you will never have too much information and knowledge in your bank "brain"!

A wise man told me once "the worker digging in the field can have the knowledge to invent a component that were change the world; he just needs the opportunity to do it!"

You can have an idea that would change lives, it just takes a lot of confidence and tunnel vision to follow it through and make it a reality.

Ron Hickman (sadly died February 2011) who invented the "Workmate" (a diy portable vice/bench) was one such inventor; he invented it 1961 and Stanley told him it would not sell in big enough volume for them, so he sold them himself!

In 1972, Black & Decker woke up to the potential and mass produced them - an estimated 30 million have since been sold.

This is just one example of ordinary people inventing extraordinary items.

We should all keep growing, moving forward and learning new information and techniques every day of our lives.

You never know when you will be presented with the opportunity to use all your knowledge for your own good and the good of the human race.

Selection (choice, options, variety, uncertainty)

Why am I bored?

"Life is either a daring adventure or nothing at all."
¯ Helen Keller, *The Open Door*

We all have a certain need for excitement and fun in our lives.

When life is going along smoothly and we have complete certainty of what is happening next we will certainly feel secure; however, after a long period of certainty boredom is liable to set in.

Some people grow up with an overdeveloped desire for uncertainty and are apt to enjoy having a gamble, taking a risk and not really counting the consequences.

As I said, there is a certain emotional need for a variety, choice, and uncertainty in our lives but this is one need that we have to be disciplined about by keeping a balance.

In business, we sometimes see directors and business owners take unreasonable risks with the decisions they make and sometimes those risks are the cause of their business failing.

Conversely, if nobody ever took a risk, new discoveries would not be made and the human race would become static.

We would probably be still living in caves if our forefathers had not taken a gamble and started to make use of all the stones and rocks available.

Likely there was an overcrowding then too; somebody had to move out and build themselves a home.

When we exercise our needs for uncertainty and choice, we are emulating the great explorers of the past who cast aside their need for certainty and eagerly embraced their emotional need for variety and uncertainty as they ventured into the unknown.

Our participation in sport is another way that we satisfy our needs for choice, variety and uncertainty. In sport, we deliberately create a situation full of uncertainty and unknown outcomes.

When we shop, even for our basic needs, we look for a selection to choose from and we get a great amount of satisfaction when we find that which we have been searching.

Even by our basic survival instincts, we desire a selection of potential mates from which to choose; a choice we will make by the influence of all our emotional needs.

The excitement of uncertainty will heighten our intensity as we search for our lifelong partner (what we hope will be a lifelong partner).

If we did not have an emotional need for uncertainty, selection, choice we would go through life without feeling any need for curiosity or excitement.

Life would be extremely dull!

Curiosity and excitement are the offshoots of the emotional need for variety, uncertainty, selection and choice.

Balance

We need all six emotional needs in our life in proper proportions.

We need to supply our needs in a balanced fashion, because if we over supply one emotional need it will knock our other emotions out of balance and more likely diminish one or more of them.

Humanity:- Compassion, Love, Understanding

Altruism:- Giving, receiving, Charity

Belief:- Confidence, self belief, certainty

Importance:- Self esteem, Significance

Transition:- Growth, Learning, Going forward

Selection:- Choice, Options, Variety

Every human needs the above components in their life. In order to maintain fulfilled relationships with others, we need to support them to have these components balanced in *their* lives.

The balance of all above emotional components is vital.

If we get one component out of balance or oversupplied, then we will find that it diminishes the other emotional needs in various ways.

Take, for instance, importance (self-esteem, significance). If you go all out for importance and significance in your life, you may find that people view you as bigheaded and possibly a bit of a show off.

This will cause you to lose their respect and love; thereby reducing your significance and importance.

If overdone, humanity may cause you to act in too humble a manner and you can become viewed as being a pushover or, as we say in the UK, "a wet blanket".

This will undermine your importance and significance.

Keeping a healthy balance is essential in all your emotional needs.

Ray Minniecon is an Aboriginal pastor with roots in the Kabikabi and Gurang-Gurang tribes of Queensland. He lives in Sydney and has dedicated his life to supporting members of the Stolen Generations of Aboriginals. The term "Stolen Generations" refers to the tens of thousands of Aboriginal children who, from the late 1800s until the 1970s, were forcibly removed from their families by government agencies and church missions in an attempt to assimilate them into the culture of white Australia.

As a child I lived in fear. My parents told me that if the police tried to pick us up we should run like crazy. There were times when the black police car would come into the missions and I'd hear women screaming from one end of the community to the other for their children to run into the bush and hide. I was one of the lucky ones who never got caught.

My father was a Christian leader who worked as a cane cutter and this gave him permission to work on cane farms throughout Queensland. So we would move with him from farm to farm, and when the cane season finished we lived back on the designated reserves or missions. In those days Aboriginal people weren't allowed into the towns.

The Aboriginal Protection Acts (which didn't protect us at all) gave the police the authority to remove Aboriginal children from their families and put them in institutional facilities or foster homes. These children later became known as the Stolen Generations and were subjected to abuse of every possible kind.

Aboriginal people had no recognition. We had never been counted in the census, so no one knew exactly how many massacres there had been. The government had control over every aspect of our life. We had to live on reserves, we weren't allowed out after 6 pm; we could not mix with white people. The government would determine if we could marry and who we could marry, how much money we had and who we could work for. We were also restricted in our capacity to get involved in any political agendas and forbidden to speak our languages or practise our traditional cultures.

Then in 1967 there was a National Referendum, called the "Yes" Vote, when Australians voted overwhelmingly to amend the constitution to include Aboriginal people in the census. The vote was supposed to make us all equal citizens and although it did bring an end to the era of false removals, it created a different set of problems.

As we came out of these reserves and foster homes we were forced to live in new urban environments where we now had to face the daily onslaught of racism. I joined the rest of the young people who didn't have the wherewithal to counteract this racism and like them found the only way to relieve the pain was to get drunk and take drugs. It was also a freedom for us. Living without restrictions, meant for the first time we could do whatever we wanted to do.

My parents were also struggling with these Issues, but what kept them together was my father's incredible faith and eventually I felt the call to follow in his footsteps and *leave behind the drug induced state I was so enjoying. I knew I had to draw back into his faith to find a different direction for my life. That's when I became politically activated. I did eight years of studying which gave me access to the records and stories of my people. I learnt about injustices that none of my community knew about because we hadn't had access to newspapers. We were blinded to the cruel actions of the Government which had been implemented with impunity.*

Once I graduated I was headhunted to go into government because I was one of the few Aboriginals with a degree, but I decided I wanted to work on the streets, at the grass roots where the greatest need lay.

The terrible pain you still see on the streets shows how the brutality of our history is continuing into the present.

Many times I've witnessed a white Australian ask a Stolen Generations member for their forgiveness, and the Stolen Generations person will then look them straight in the eye and say "You can't apologise if you weren't directly responsible. The Government knew what they were doing. They are the guilty ones." There was an apology in a sense. Kevin Rudd, the Australian Prime Minister in 2008, apologised on behalf of all Australians following a national "Sorry" movement. Whilst many of the promises the Government made have not been implemented, it pricked the conscience of a nation and was a turning point. When someone says "I'm sorry" then something changes in your spirit.

Healing is a meaningless word for Aboriginal people because we possess a wound that cannot be healed. Rape of the soul is so profound - and particularly for the Stolen Generations who were forcibly removed from their parents, communities, and culture. You can't put a band aid on that. For these people the concept of healing, and the concept of forgiveness is difficult. Reconciliation only happens when you're restored in your own spirit. That's why we prefer to talk about emotional and psychological well-being. If you fix the psyche and restore wellbeing through a process of reconnection and reconstruction of identity, then you. have a platform for someone to deal with intergenerational pain and be a human being again. Only then can someone have an opportunity to receive or express forgiveness.

I struggle with forgiveness but I know I have to practise it every day to relieve my bitterness. It's a moment by moment thing because I can walk into a shop and have a person do racist acts without even knowing they are racist. And when that happens I have to walk away and deal with my rage and anger, and learn to say "okay Ray, forgive that person". If I didn't forgive then the past would always be present.

The above story has been republished by kind permission of the "Forgiveness Project" www.theforgivenessproject.com

Abuse help coaching-
http://www.TomMcAbuseRecoveryCoach.co.uk

http://tinyurl.com/j34asab (TomMc ARC)

Chapter 6

Victor or victim? Which do you want to be?

Can you afford not to forgive?

This is a question that we cannot really answer truthfully until we are in possession of the full facts of what forgiving entails and the benefits or pitfalls.

Many people will regard forgiveness as a weakness while others consider it not only a virtue but also an act of wisdom.

That may seem a bit of a far out statement but after we reviewed the pros and cons of forgiving we may then come back to this question and be more enlightened and able to give an honest answer.

Is forgiveness a sign of weakness or strength?

Does it open us up to more violation or will it in some way help us become immune to our aggressors.

Our willingness to forgive may be seen by our tormentors as an indication that their aggression is not having the desired effect on us.

In this way forgiveness is strength!

189

In contrast, we may be viewed as weak and vulnerable when we are always willing to accept being insulted, humiliated or violated in any way.

However, we can counteract this perceived weakness by learning to become more immune to people who try to violate us simply by not letting their words damage our dignity and self-respect.

In nearly all cases of abuse or harassment, it is our dignity and self-respect that is the most damaged.

To recover from this, we need to build up our self-confidence and self-esteem by various ways as discussed in this book.

When we look at the harshest and most demeaning acts of abuse, especially abuse endured during childhood, then we will realize that there are few real avenues of recovery available.

One of those avenues is definitely the way of forgiveness.

Forgiving heals the forgiver!

You cannot afford not to forgive!

Before we go forward to forgive, we have first to recognize what forgiveness means.

What is forgiveness?

This is the Oxford Thesaurus explanation of forgiveness!

Forgiveness is pardon, absolution, exoneration, remission, dispensation, indulgence, clemency, mercy; reprieve, amnesty;

That is just about every magnanimous action that can be named.

I would say that is unilateral forgiveness; in other words, complete forgiveness without regard for the circumstances.

When we take into consideration our six emotional needs and consider charity as one of them, forgiveness could be viewed as the ultimate charity towards another.

However, to demand forgiveness will be the exact opposite of charity because in fairness forgiveness can require an enormous amount of effort and soul-searching.

This may sound like a paradox; however, if an individual is willing to forgive without being put under pressure, they will be demonstrating great charity and courage.

To expect forgiveness in extreme cases of heinous abuse would seem to be a step too far.

As we go forward and look at the benefits of forgiving to the forgiver, we can review and assess the options available to them.

We will review those benefits later on.

Let us consider an almost undisputed fact that all of us have at some time something to forgive, some slight or offence by others with trivial or major significance.

In all cases, the severity of the offence by others will be evaluated by our own emotional response to the incident.

We can use our confidence and sense of self-worth to isolate ourselves from our feeling of indignation and damage to our dignity and self-respect.

In this way, we can trivialize the incident and refuse to allow it to have a severe impact on our ego.

However, if our confidence and self-esteem is low, then all those words of criticism and disrespect will have a very hurtful effect on us.

We will then become a victim to anger and resentment both of which will drag us down and if we let those feelings fester and remain they will damage our life.

We can find ourselves descending into depression and experience all the horrible feelings described earlier in this book.

"The weak can never forgive. Forgiveness is an attribute of the strong"

Mahatma Gandhi

Our first step towards forgiveness is to forgive ourselves, and this can become a major issue.

You may feel guilty about something you have done or have failed to do in the past.

Forgiving yourself is a major step in changing your life and changing how you feel about yourself.

If you have a feeling of loathing and guilt about what you have done in the past it will paralyse you and keep you static in your life. It may cause you to do things that will make your life unbearable.

In many circumstances, people with addictions have become hooked on substances in an effort to mask their pain of guilt and self-loathing that they carry as a result of past events.

There is only one proven way out; to forgive yourself and anyone else involved.

When the thoughts of the past and what you have done are circulating in your head, you will find that those thoughts will not subside or lose their power over you until you decide to forgive yourself.

Are you taking into account your mindset at the time of the occurrence of what you consider your guilty actions?

Were you guided by outside influence or others power at the time of the incident?

What if your lack of decision was due to something outside your control?

Did you consider at the time that the action or decision you took on the circumstances was for the good of all concerned?

If you knew what you know now would you have done what you did?

If you knew what your six emotional needs were and how your thought processes work as you do now, would you still have done what you did?

Take responsibility for your actions and pledge to never repeat them.

We all make mistakes, some of which are heavy and may be injuring to others, leaving us with a lasting feeling of guilt.

When we forgive ourselves, we will lessen our feeling of guilt but not our responsibility to learn from, and not repeat, our mistake.

Whatever the circumstances and however guilty you feel, the only way forward is to forgive yourself.

The past is the past; you cannot change it once it has happened.

Start forgiving yourself by taking small steps; steps like repeating I forgive myself, I am healed!

Do this several times each day.

Take one step towards forgiving yourself each day and you will quickly feel the pain of your anger; consequently, the feelings of guilt will diminish.

As you forgive yourself, the emotional grip that your guilt has on you will be lessened and your state will become more and more upbeat.

There is no other way to get healing from your emotional stress.

Forgiveness is rare.

Few people ever consider forgiving either themselves or others; it takes deep reflection and strong humanity to even consider forgiving especially others that have offended and wronged you in some severe way.

It takes courage to forgive.

Refusing to forgive will waste our lives and hold us in the limbo of our anger and resentment; causing us to suffer both mentally and physically.

We suffer physically because the state of our minds affects our physique. When our emotional state is at rock bottom, our immune system becomes impaired.

Our anger and resentment, feelings of guilt and all the emotional stress we carry within ourselves when we do not forgive builds up and leaves us with continual stress.

It is well known that stress is a cause of everyday illnesses, especially high blood pressure (which can lead to heart attacks) and ulcerated stomach.

Are you willing to waste more energy and time on your bottled-up anger and resentment or just decide to go forward and forgive and taste the freedom that forgiveness gives.

Is it necessary to get an apology from those you are forgiving?

Receiving an apology may help you come to terms with your injury and hurt. Moreover, it may encourage your abuser to have some remorse; however, forgiveness will have a far greater benefit for you if you do not base it on the condition that your abuser is contrite for the offence.

You have no power over your abuser and how they will think; you will have however full control over your own mind and by committing to forgiving you will be weakening the continued power your abuser has over you through your pain of resentment and anger.

Considering the ferocity or evilness of the violation, is it forgivable?

You do not have to agree or condone the evil done to you to be able to forgive!

Do not forgive for the other person's sake; forgiving is for your benefit and peace of mind.

One human emotional need is compassion and compassion is necessary for forgiveness.

Forgiveness does not mean forgetting, or that forgetting is necessary to forgiveness.

When you are angry with others you cannot be at peace and be compassionate to yourself; when you are not compassionate and loving to yourself you cannot love anybody else.

This will have a devastating effect on your life.

Remember my quotation:

"You have to give before you get!"
If you cannot give love you will never get love!

Forgiveness is like an antibiotic that you feed to your mind to cure the pain of resentment and anger and program your subconscious.

It counteracts the poisoning within your mind, which is slowly pulling you down and paralyzing your efforts to move towards happiness.

Lack of forgiveness will affect your physical health as well as your mind and it will also affect your future relationships.

When we hold the emotions of resentment, anger and thoughts of revenge, our emotional needs become unbalanced; thereby affecting how we interact and react to all situations in our future relationships.

To make any relationship run harmoniously, we must have our emotional needs in balance and be able to look realistically at our own needs and those of others within our relationships.

Until you come to terms with your emotions, you will be unable to trust or confidently love another human being as your hurt and pain will colour your thoughts about others that you meet.

Being unable to trust others because of the treatment we have received and our long-held emotional pain will prevent us from enjoying normal healthy relationships with others.

Forgiving will help to heal yourself even if you are forgiving an act by someone no longer living, the mere act of forgiving will set you free.

Forgiving is not excusing because the act of excusing in fact implies that the wrongdoing in the first place was not the offenders fault so therefore there is no wrong to forgive.

Forgiveness is not condoning the wrongdoing.

Forgiveness may not result in reconciliation but will help in reconciliation and restoration of the victim's emotional health.

Forgiveness is a process of overcoming anger, resentment and vengeful thoughts.

The power of forgiveness is not only dependent on feeling good because of personal moral satisfaction, but also weakens the power of the resentment and anger felt by the offended individual.

Through forgiveness we demonstrate our strength of character and courage.

Forgiveness cannot be an effective healing remedy for the emotional damage anger and resentment are causing unless all thoughts of revenge are relinquished.

Is self-forgiveness necessary?

Are we really guilty or just ignorant of the true reasons for the actions or lack of actions for which we hold ourselves accountable?

Is refusing to forgive helping you?

Is it helping your violator?

What would you gain from forgiving yourself and your enemies?

It's your decision; be a victor or victim?

Does forgiveness work?

Peace is the payback for forgiveness!

Less stress!

Can we limit our exposure to hurt?

As children we will not have knowledge or understanding of how to ward off or lessen the effect of verbal abuse and extreme criticism.

As we grow older if we are lucky we can learn to shield ourselves from insults by taking on board the advice given in the following quotation:

"People can only hurt you if you allow them to!"

Is refusing to forgive wasting our life and holding us in limbo?

Your enemy will retain power over you until you forgive them.

You have a choice to forgive or not forgive.

You forgive for yourself not for somebody else.

When thinking of forgiveness we may be inclined to think of justice.

Justice can get mixed up with revenge and, when it does, it also becomes an emotion that creates a lasting and painful feeling. Again, this feeling will be hard to get rid of without applying the medicine of "forgiveness".

My thoughts on revenge are that revenge is more harmful to the avenger than to the recipient.

If you seek revenge you may well end up becoming even more of a victim by earning a criminal record and possibly ending up in prison.

That would compound the harm already done to you by your violators and possibly ruin you for the rest of your life.

Forgiveness is taught by most religions and is rooted in centuries of wisdom.

In the Christian religion forgiveness is extensively promoted as virtue.

"Forgive them for they know not what they do" (Jesus on the cross).

For all religions and people of non-religion, I am sure forgiveness will be viewed as a sensible approach to life.

Forgiveness is an internal thing and is done for one's own healing and not exclusively for the good of those we are forgiving.

By the fact that we decided to forgive we are allowing ourselves to let go of the familiar if painful emotional feelings that have been a constant part of our lives.

Even pain can become a recognized part of our lives and we may have fears of the unknown when we contemplate eliminating the pain.

This may sound unbelievable but it can be true; take for instance an alcoholic or a drug addict. Despite having the opportunity to free themselves of the slavery of their addiction, they will hesitate because of moving out of their comfort zone and that with which they are familiar. They will feel almost a sense of bereavement as their addiction has become a constant companion.

Until forgiveness is implemented victims will find themselves indefinitely under the power of their abusers.

Forgive and move on with your life!

Not only will forgiveness help you to move on with your life it will enable you to become happy and enjoy your future.

Happiness?

Do you know what happiness is?

When we try to define happiness, we must first realize that everyone has a different perception of the concept.

The state that you consider is happiness may be viewed as one of distress by the next person. You will review what you consider to be happiness in line with your principles, your values and your cultural upbringing.

You may consider being happy requires wealth and having all of the good things in life freely available to you. I am sure you would be able to name many people who to your knowledge are quite wealthy and to all outward signs have everything they need in life.

Can you say that they are happy and feel fulfilled in life?

Having great wealth should undoubtedly make you feel comfortable and secure in life. You will also need the security of knowing that you are within a loving circle of friends and family.

I believe that any person who can say with confidence that they have at least three and if they are extremely fortunate up to five people in their life of whom they can say "I can trust this person with my life". That person should be truly happy even if they have barely enough wealth to see them through the next six months.

Another great benchmark of happiness is the state of your health, assuming you are in good health and you are living in circumstances whereby you can maintain your health by good diet and exercise, then you are truly fortunate.

Remembering always that most things that happens to us, is our responsibility we should always be vigilant about maintaining good health and then if we are unfortunate to be afflicted with ill-health of any sort we have the consolation of knowing that it is not our own fault.

You will have your own way of pursuing happiness and providing you ensure that you do not harm yourself or others in the pursuit then you can feel justified in whatever way you do it.

Many people consider they are not happy until they are heavily intoxicated or they have numbed their brains with some drug or other. I would be completely out of order if I did not say that I consider this to be completely wrong. There are two basic reasons why anyone does anything:

1. to avoid pain
2. to gain pleasure

Sadly, some people take pleasure in harming others, either physically or emotionally. Because they are emotionally damaged in some way, they think this will make them happy. Those people are basically "bullies" and are lacking in confidence and self-esteem. In such cases, these people are in need of professional help.

Pleasure is experienced in the pursuit of happiness; for example, when we go on holidays we gain pleasure as we enjoy the beach, the countryside, or perhaps skiing or having a round of golf.

Those are all pleasurable pursuits and, in most cases, very healthy ones that will take us towards the state of happiness.

Engaging in one's hobby or sport is another healthy way of gaining happiness.

Your attitude towards life is another important factor as to how happy your state in life is going to be. With a positive and optimistic attitude you are undoubtedly well on your way to happiness.

If you give way to negativity and being always pessimistic and stressed about the future then you are going to have great difficulty achieving happiness.

Quotation:-

"Laugh and the world laugh you - cry and you cry alone!"

Sad, but unfortunately it is usually true!

Being under a cloud of emotional anger and resentment that is being carried over from a period of abuse or mistreatment is a guarantee of losing out on happiness.

For this pain "forgiveness" is the medicine to take it away!

It may be seen as disrespectful to call this emotional anger and pain a "baggage" that is carried by the victim; however it is indeed a heavy load and worth taking the forgiveness medicine for ease of the weight on one's heart and the pain of the memories.

On many occasions, the help and encouragement of a coach can be of benefit; knowing that someone who cares is there to support you.

Abuse help coaching-
http://www.TomMcAbuseRecoveryCoach.co.uk

http://tinyurl.com/j34asab (TomMc ARC)

Forgiving will also bring a sense of peace into your life.

Peace!

Unconsciously, most people are unaware of whether or not it is important to live in peace.

The media, government and many groups in our society do not support the idea of living in peace and harmony; therefore, it is not easy for most individuals to grasp the concept that peace is the only true path for humans to follow in order to survive as a race.

Most governments proclaim that their legislation and strategies are geared to promotion of peace.

This is debatable.

We need to look to our own behaviour and our interaction with others and ask ourselves are our actions and communications steering our lives towards peace.

If your actions do not promote peace then you need to modify your attitude in general and temper your life with compassion.

If you are not a peaceful person and have turmoil and problems with others in your life, then it is probably your fault that you have not peace and comfort in your life.

Some people can start mini wars in their lives over the most trivial things.

A war in your life can be as simple as picking on someone who you feel is weaker than you, or someone who feels you are weaker than them actually picking on you.

If you see any one weaker and less able to defend themselves against bullies or aggression and you do not try to make peace then you are as guilty as the one that is doing the bullying.

If you condone someone who is wrong in their actions, aggressive, abusive or picking on someone physically or mentally, then you are guilty of promoting this particular "war"

You should always be a peacemaker.

Being a peacemaker, whether it is your war or someone else's, takes significant technique and levelheadedness.

Most people in disagreement or "war" as we have called it are certain that they are in the "right" and the other party is the guilty one.

To bring peace to the situation both parties will have to gain some credit and at the same time to admit some guilt for the situation as it is.

The following is one technique to try to resolve the disagreement between parties.

1. Have each person state their side of the dispute and state it back to them, and have them agree on what is said. It is useful to write down the statement.
2. Next you read the statement of one person to the opposite person in the dispute and ask them if they understand what has been stated.
3. Do not allow them to dispute at this point. Get an agreement of understanding from them.
4. Do the same with both people.

212

5. Get an agreement on as many points as possible on both statements from both people and then endeavour to get a peaceful agreement.

If you submit to a bully, you will never achieve peace from them. They will perceive that you as weaker and will feed on their own lack of self-esteem by continuing to make you a victim.

In most cases, the bullies want to increase their perceived power in their community and build up their ego. The reason for this is simply because they feel inferior and want to make themselves feel better.

Their plan will become worthless when you refuse to become a victim and expose them for what they are.

Even if you use passive resistance, you will be showing that you are capable of resisting and will continue to do so.

By the same token, the more you resist the more confident you will become and when they see this, your abusers own feeling of confidence will start to suffer and you can gradually become stronger in their eyes.

No matter what the situation in your life, always stick to your principles and your beliefs.

This will give you more confidence in yourself and for what you stand for enabling you to build stronger self-esteem.

Finding peace may not come easy and you may have to remove yourself from certain situations and certain people who are causing you grief and denying you peace in your life.

Depending on where you live and the prevailing culture in your community, you may even have to remove yourself from your own environment and disassociate yourself from people who you have known and grown-up with.

This is unfortunately the case for some people who have grown up in a community with a "gang" culture.

It may be heart-wrenching, but it may be the only way to bring peace to your life!

As regards "gang" culture – I will mention one observation I received from one of my clients.

This young man had done some very violent things in his youth and was feeling very guilty about them.

He took on the idea of forgiving oneself and having thought deeply on his actions he decided that at the time of his actions he was not fully aware of the damage and the enormity of what he was doing.

Because of his guilty conscience about those incidents and other things in his life he had been self harming and leading a very chaotic lifestyle.

When the idea of forgiveness was presented to him, he gave it full consideration.

Forgiveness is not just for people who have been abused and mistreated, it is also for those who have reformed and want to repay their debt to society.

With forgiveness your success is indeed possible!

One of the most fundamental needs in your life has to be your desire to strive continually for success and achieve your goals and dreams.

This, with your continued desire to improve your environment and the lot of your fellow human beings, is an essential part of the attitude necessary for continued success and continued feeling of fulfillment in your life.

When this continual desire becomes a natural feeling, you will know that your subconscious mindset is anchored successfully in the right direction.

When you look elsewhere in this book at the meaning of success, you will realise that everybody's concept of success is inherently different.

For some people their desire for success will not be satisfied until they are extremely rich financially, while for others success can mean happiness in the state they are in and with the material and health sources that they presently have.

If you are one of the former one's who will not consider themselves successful until they are extremely rich, this mindset can leave you emotionally and spiritually unsettled and very stressed.

There is no shame in wanting to be extremely rich. But abandoning all other desires in life apart from getting rich can leave you leading a very impoverished life emotionally and spiritually.

There are some extremely rich people in this world who do fantastically credible and generous works with their wealth.

Bill Gates, Richard Branson and at least a dozen more leaders in industrial have contributed to the improvement in the lives of many in the Third World and poor communities elsewhere. They have launched projects in health and welfare that is extremely beneficial to several poorer communities. They have contributed to both health and education in Africa and elsewhere.

Spending your life and your career working solely for monetary gain without all the other good things in life is hardly a great way to use up your time in this life, taking note that you have only one life to lead and you will never get another chance to have a happy existence.

The story of Scrooge is repeated every Christmas and it is a story worthy of our full attention.

If you are not happy within yourself, of whom you are, what you are, what you represent to the world and how contented and confident you are about your integrity and character no amount of money or material wealth will buy you a happy life. When you build a character for yourself that is full of integrity, honesty and humanity you will justifiably feel your self-esteem soar and your confidence grow steadily as you gain your success in life.

Your success is definitely achievable and if what you do in life is in line with your principles, your values and your passions then you will have a successful and joyous life. When you share what you have in life and help someone else get what they want then your satisfaction in your successes will be multiplied hundreds if not thousands of times.

Your satisfaction in the successes of life will come from within you and you will not rely on outside influences and outside stimulants to make you happy.

I truly believe that this is the reason why so many successful young people, instead of looking inside their own emotional feelings for happiness and enjoyment they look outwards for external stimulants like drugs and alcohol to give them the "good feeling" syndrome.

I will give you two quotations that I believe contain an enormous amount of the truth!

"You have to give before you get!"

"Everything you give to others doubles in value!"

When you gain the experience of success, even if it is only a small success it will galvanize you and energies you to go forward to bigger successes; that is, success breeds success. You will begin to recognize yourself as a person who is accustomed to being successful in whatever you do and to expect success each day.

This should become second nature to you and be part of your character.

This mindset will act as a magnet to attract success in all parts of your life.

To sustain the success you will have to follow the example above, where your follow your career in strict line with your principles and values and are willing to share your material success and your emotional success with others in order to help them also to achieve what they desire in life.

This will enable you to access what is the true meaning of life; the fulfilling experience of helping others achieve what they desire in their life.

When you achieve this fulfillment you will never have to look outside of yourself for anything to make you feel good spiritually and emotionally; therefore, you will never have to look for outside stimulation like drugs or alcohol.

When you have honest success in your life where you have fulfillment and joy in your life, perhaps sharing it with a loved one and family then you will have achieved the ultimate ambition of contributing to the human race.

This is what we were all put on Earth for and until we progress in some way towards this end we will not feel at ease with ourselves

Everyone was born to make a difference, a difference that most people believe they cannot make, believing that because they are not famous or extremely rich that they are not capable of touching others lives in a beneficial way.

Most people do not realize that it is very easy to contribute to other people's state in this life.

Consider, how much of a change in a emotion you can achieve by just a simple "hello" to someone you meet who may at that moment feel very down or could perhaps be without any friends.

As you go through your day you may pass a homeless person or someone looking for some pennies, simply to buy themselves some food, and your "hello" and perhaps a little donation can make a world of difference in the person's life.

Both you and they will feel emotional benefit from the interaction.

If you repeat this a few times it can gradually become a habit and you may well feel that you are justified in striving for richness when you are happy to share your good fortune with others who are less fortunate than you.

You know that your success is indeed possible, and when you pursue it in line with your principles and values having set your goals and dreams to coincide with your passion, undoubtedly your success will be achievable and sustainable.

When you employ forgiveness you will be opening the gateway to gain confidence in your life.

Here are some ways to help you gain confidence:

Within your community or your circle of friends you will be able to identify one individual that you admire and respect and would like to have the same confidence and self-esteem that this person processes.

In fact you may even consider this person as one of your heroes. Providing this person is of extremely good character and is not just a shallow individual like some celebrities are, then you will benefit by modeling yourself on this person.

You can adopt this person's body language and their way of interaction with others.

This is called modeling and it is a useful way of increasing your confidence and helping you to be less sensitive and less easily embarrassed.

Be aware of how you present yourself each day and always try to be cheerful and pleasant to everybody you meet. Always remember my quotation:-

"What you present to others will be reflected back to you"

Even when you are feeling a little bit down and it may take a very big effort it is always worthwhile to try and not spoil other people's day by looking really glum.

You have learned many things in the past and no matter what the present situation is you will have an answer in your subconscious so do not let yourself get into a state of stress over any problem no matter how severe it may seem.

Instead of stressing over a situation, stop and work out a plan for resolving the issues.

Most problems will seem very small indeed in six months' time.

Do not stress and worry, just plan a resolution for your problem!

Treat yourself to something that cheers you up like new clothes or if you are a lady have you hair done.

This will raise your spirits and no matter what your problems or how low your confidence is, you will feel much better about yourself after you pamper yourself.

As you go through life, always plan ahead and be prepared for whatever challenges you are about face.

Every day you will meet new problems and challenges, it may be an interview for a new job, a difficult problem at work or a difficult manager or boss that you have to contend would each day, but if you put a plan of action in place you will be prepared and life will go much more smoothly.

As your life improves so will your confidence and self-esteem!

You will know what you are good at and, as often as you can, engage in the activities and the work for which your skills are designed.

In this way, you will find that life is much smoother and you will be a happier person. With happiness comes enhanced confidence and self-esteem.

You will unfortunately be aware of your weaknesses and may even worry about them occasionally.

Knowing your weakness is halfway to curing it, as most people are unaware of their weaknesses and continue through life compounding their weaknesses instead of eliminating them.

When you recognize your weaknesses, it is a good plan to write them down and then work out how you can eliminate them.

Make one column for your weaknesses and another column on how to eliminate them and make them into strengths.

If one of your weaknesses is being too generous (it is a virtue to be generous) and overanxious to help people even when they don't need help, then it is time for you to learn how to say "no"

Many people you meet will take advantage of you if you are a generous person and just keep taking without giving anything back.

It is no crime to say "no" and in fact you may be help them more by saying "no" than if you conceded to the request.

When you "over help" some people you take away their ability and initiative to help themselves. In other words you disenable them.

No matter what the challenge or undertaking that you are about to embark on you should always go forward with a positive "**I can do**" attitude.

Be aware of all that you have accomplished during your life and know that you can succeed whatever the challenge.

Be aware that whatever project or undertaking you set out on when you set your mind on success and summons up a positive attitude you are more than halfway to success.

Success is achieved in the mind first and then in reality.

Do not ever entertain a negative attitude or allow yourself to have negative thoughts about your abilities your skills or your esteem.

Negative targets go around in circles and those circles increase every time you go around i.e. you get in a Catch-22 situation - **negativity breeds negativity!**

Stop yourself right away if you are having a negative thought and ask yourself is this relevant. Is it really important in the overall scheme of things?

Do not beat yourself up over little things and do not let your self feel "little" either. You have the core of greatness in your DNA, just like everybody else. All the great historical characters were just normal human beings like you and me!

Do not allow others' comments or criticisms pull you down. Do not let them have power over you as you are free human being and are unique in all respects.

Other people may think that the way you lead your life and operate is not to their liking but with all due respect perhaps they are not perfect either. If they were confident and had strong self esteem, they would not feel compelled to comment on you.

Remember, others can only hurt you if you give them your consent to do so! In other words if you allow their comments to hurt you and pull you down then you are giving them permission to do you harm.

No one can make you feel inferior without your consent. (Eleanor Roosevalt)

When I was going to school we had a saying:-

"Sticks and stones will break my bones but words won't do me any harm!"

We need to develop a belief that nasty words of criticism cannot get through to us and we can shake them off like water off a ducks back.

I will insert a little parable here:

One day a farmer's donkey fell down into a well. The animal cried for hours as the farmer tried to figure out what to do. Finally, he decided the animal was old, and the well needed to be covered up anyway; it just wasn't worth   it   to   retrieve   the   donkey.

He invited all his neighbors to come over and shovel

dirt into the well. At first, the donkey realized what was happening and cried horribly. Then, to everyone's amazement, he quieted down.

A few shovel loads later, the farmer looked down the well. He was astonished at what he saw. With each shovel of dirt that hit his back, the donkey was doing something amazing. He would shake it off and take a step up...

As the farmer's neighbors continued to shovel dirt on top of the animal, he would shake it off and take a step up. Pretty soon, everyone was amazed as the donkey stepped up over the edge of the well, and happily trotted off! ***

Life is going to shovel dirt on you, all kinds of dirt. The trick to getting out of the hole is to shake it off and take a step up. Each of our troubles is a stepping stone. We can get out of the deepest holes just by not stopping, never giving up! Shake it off and take a step up.

Make a list of words that come to mind when you are annoyed or when you feel let down.

You will use different words to mean the same thing and depending upon how strong or how much emotional impact each word has, the word you use will affect your reaction to the situation.

Instead of saying "I am furious about this", perhaps "I am slightly annoyed" will take the anger out of the situation.

That is just one example and if you look for less emotional words when you think of how you feel then your feelings will improve!

A useful way to improve your confidence and self-esteem is to list your successes and what you have done during the day that has made you feel good about yourself.

The more successes you have, it becomes like taking a tonic to build your strength in confidence and self-esteem.

Do not short change yourself when giving yourself credit for your achievements. Ensure you review each little success, especially when you have done something that benefits someone else.

Always feel gratitude for the good things you have in life, like the people who love you, the people you love and the people you can rely on for help when you need them.

You know all those people are and you can think about them in a warm, graciously way and appreciate that you are surrounded by a supporting circle.

If you are unfortunately without a supporting circle then I am sure there is at least one person you can look to for help when needed.

Every morning a useful practice is to review the events of the coming day and plan ahead for how you are going to handle each situation to ensure that you have a successful outcome.

Run the video in your mind of you handling all situations in a confident and successful manner. You will find that this will give you a confident edge as you go through your day.

As you progress through your day, be aware of how you carry yourself; in other words, hold your head up high and look everybody straight in the eye. Walk with purpose and do not drag your feet.

Always look as if you are on a mission and you know exactly where you are going.

You may not feel 100% confident, but looking confident is the first step.

When you move around consistently, you create energy and confidence; thereby equipping you to tackle whatever problems you encounter.

Remember that motion creates emotion!

Stay in motion and your emotions will be creative and progressive.

Do not be shy of bragging about yourself and your achievements.

You are a unique and worthy individual and should feel proud of your achievements. Do not hesitate to let people know the extent of your capabilities.

There is no harm in indulging in a little self-publicity, just do not overdo it as it then becomes "boasting" and people who boast are seldom liked.

You only pass this way but once so live life to the full and do not worry about little annoyances and small problems. Just remember in 10 or 20 years time, you will probably be unable to remember those little problems!

Live life to the full and remember you only live once - this is not a rehearsal!!!

To go forward with your life -

You cannot afford not to forgive!

Starting again is only possible if you forgive.

Use the "forgiveness medicine" to take away the pain!"

To help you forgive consider the following points.

1 Your emotions

Anger, hatred and resentment are all feelings that stay with you for years from the time that you endured your injustices and indignities.

Those damaging emotions are causing a continual degrading effect on you even many years afterwards and may unbeknown to you causing you to hold back from going forward and getting your deserved results in your life.

Those feelings will not only damage you emotionally, they will manifest in your physical state also and can be a major cause in your state of health.

Your emotions have a direct impact on your physique. In plain language, the mind controls the body!

2 Your loss

When you were abused or violated you lost your dignity and feelings of self worth leaving you feeling unloved and unwanted. Feeling loved is a major need of all humans young or old and if one has love taken away when a child or young adult, it is an almost insurmountable task to restore confidence and self-esteem.

Added to this tragedy is the sad reality that a large number of victims will have sought emotional pain relief in drugs and/or alcohol; thereby giving them another group of problems.

When all this is reviewed and weighed up, it is easy to be disbelieving when forgiveness is proposed as a means of easing your emotional stress; however, it has a proven success rate (see chapter 3).

3 Need for understanding

Let's look at something that is going to very painful for most - the mindset of bullies.

When we think of bullying, it is usual for a picture to appear in our mind off a bigger kid picking on a smaller one in the schoolyard.

A bully's mindset is not always obvious to people at large.

Bullies suffer from low self-confidence and are boosting their ego to make themselves feel good by picking on people who are weaker, possibly both physically and mentally.

This is mostly the case but not always, some bullies are overconfident and do not realize that they are doing wrong.

Most teenage and adult victims of bullying usually suffer themselves from low confidence and their tormentors usually see or sense this and recognise that they are easy victims.

Bullies are usually very quick to notice potential victims who are low in self confidence and demonstrate this by their body language and their approach to others.

The victims will quickly lose whatever confidence they have as they are constantly attacked.

When a victim picks up the courage to defend themselves, in most cases, the bullies immediately back off and do not try to push their luck again.

This was true not just for schoolyard bullies but for bullies in the work place and the home.

If you have any suspicion that your child is being bullied, you should do whatever you can to protect them and preserve their self-confidence.

In many cases, your child will be reluctant to confide in you about being bullied, or you may not be aware of the situation yourself.

If your child starts to behave suspiciously, appears with cuts and bruises that they cannot explain, or starts to exhibit a withdrawn and secretive personality, then there are grounds to be suspicious and suspect that they are being bullied.

With compassion; understanding and gentle coaxing, you should be able to discover the truth.

Bullies will only have as much power as the victim will allow them!

Your child should understand that bullies are completely wrong and that it is okay and proper to "tell on them" - grass them up.

Your child may be in fear of reprisals and further bullying, and will be very reluctant to name their tormentor; therefore your reassurance of support is very important.

You must get other adults involved as your child's teachers and other parents, in order to ensure other children do not also become victims.

If a bully is physically threatening your child and your school's efforts are ineffective, it may become necessary for your child to be taught to defend themselves.

A martial arts course will be very beneficial and will provide the skills to build up your child's confidence.

When a child becomes competent in defending themselves, they may find that they will not have to use their new-found skills. This is because the bully will be deterred by their new-found confidence.

A self-defense program can be a good path to take towards building self-confidence, both for adults and children.

Cyber-bullying is another form that has become more prevalent in recent years.

Bullies who use cyber-bullying techniques are encouraged by the fact that they may remain unknown to the victims, due to the anonymity of the Internet.

All bullies will focus on their victim's emotions and build on the fact that the victim will be unwilling to part from their friends.

It is also extensively used by girls who tend to call each other "names" and criticize the victim's appearance and looks.

In most cases, the bullies are underachievers while the bullied are children who are forging forward with their education.

Again, this proves that bullies are people of low self-esteem who are just trying to boost their ego.

Bullying does not go away when we become adults.

There are manipulative, abusive and sometimes evil people in the adult working world also.

You may have a co- worker who cons you into doing the work for them or your boss who simply overwhelms you with work and threatens you if you do not do it.

Be assertive and stand up for yourself. If it continues, report them to a higher authority.

Be assured that bullies, regardless of age, are people with very low self-esteem. Once you gain the confidence to confront them, inform them, their behaviour is no longer acceptable. They will back down and leave you alone.

They can only draw the power from you that they desire if you allow them to do so.

239

Many bullies may themselves be the victims of bullying, perhaps in their own homes if they are children or have been bullied as children themselves.

Unfortunately, they may believe that this is normal in life as they have not experienced any different.

They need educating on normal conduct and how to interact with their peers.

Their ignorance may somewhat mitigate their despicable conduct but it does not completely excuse it.

4 Need for love

Most people have several different ways of understanding love, and it is not easy to state exactly what love is.

A quote here from the Road Less Travelled by M Scott Peck on "love"

Love is "The will to extend oneself for the purpose of nurturing one's own or another's spiritual growth"

(M. Scott Peck: THE ROAD LESS TRAVELLED (Simon & Schuster, 1978). First published in Great Britain by Hutchinson & Co in 1983. Reissued in Great Britain by Arrow Books in 2006. Copyright © 1978 M. Scott Peck.)

Personally, I would add "material growth" as well as spiritual.

The way I understand it is that when we love others we are concerned for their welfare, both materially and spiritually.

First and foremost, we must love ourselves. If we do not love and respect ourselves, we cannot have the capacity to love anyone else.

Until we learn to love ourselves, we will never be capable of loving anyone else.

People who are continually having disagreements and ill feeling with others are people who are incapable of loving themselves; therefore, they cannot love or appreciate anyone else.

The love we have for our partners, family and siblings will be more acute and fervent than the love we show for our other fellow humans.

Nevertheless, when we express concern for the rest of humanity, we are showing a degree of love with which we were all born.

When we deny this love, which is merely human nature, we can easily let destructive emotions into our lives; for example, jealousy and hatred.

Without love and compassion, we are just empty shells. Irrespective of the great heights of wealth we achieve, we will never feel true contentment and happiness unless we are willing and eager to share our good fortune with others.

5 What will it cost you?

Being a victim of abuse and violation will have a devastating emotional effect that will cause dysfunction and inability to achieve in one's life.

The continual painful emotional memories must be weakened and toned down to enable any reasonable state of existence.

242

The only way to achieve this is to embark on the pathway of forgiveness.

6 Forgiveness.

I will repeat the instructions for the "Burn Your Past" exercise in chapter three.

If you failed to do the exercise, I urge you to do it now!

Burn Your Past!

Get a few sheets of paper to write on.

This next action may cause you some pain; however, it is worth the effort.

Put your mind into a state of forgiveness - at least think about forgiving.

Now the painful part; cast your mind back to your ordeal and write everything you remember about the event or events that caused you so much pain.

Write everything; do not leave out any detail.

When you have written every last horror, your emotional feelings and your physical feelings experienced at the time, take them to somewhere safe (like the kitchen sink) and...

BURN THEM!!

Watch them burn with this thought in your mind:

That is the end of my torture – I have forgiven and my past abusers, tormentors and violators can no longer cause me pain!!

I am FREE!

Install a trigger – grip your right wrist with your left hand (or the opposite way, whatever feels most comfortable to you) as you watch the papers burn during the above exercise.

If you ever find yourself slipping towards your bad feelings again, repeat the trigger and you will remember the emotions you had when you did the "Burning your past" exercise!

Take a deep, deep breath and let yourself feel good with a warm glow spreading through your body and the above thought repeating in your mind –

That is the end of my torture – I have forgiven and my past abusers, tormentors and violators can no longer cause me pain!!

I am FREE!

A new beginning!

When coming to terms with your past, it is very helpful to seek the help of a mentor or coach who will encourage you in your endeavours to change your life.

See my coaching tips and information at:

http://www.TomMcAbuseRecoveryCoach.co.uk

A new beginning is always possible no matter how far down the road you have travelled, and no matter what pain or disappointment you have faced. As long as you are still breathing, there is no limit to what you can achieve. Be a victor not a victim!

"All people are capable of being perpetrators or victims - and sometimes both."

*After Father Michael Lapsley was exiled by the South African Government in 1976, he joined the African National Congress (ANC) and became one of their chaplains. Whilst living in Zimbabwe he discovered he was on the South African Government hit list. In April 1990 he received a letter bomb in the post. He now runs the **Institute for Healing of Memories** in Cape Town. He has also written a book about his experiences: **Redeeming the Past: My Journey from Freedom Fighter to Healer.***

No one told me why I was being exiled. But as a university chaplain, and in the wake of the Soweto uprising (when students were being detained and tortured) I was no friend to the apartheid regime. In exile I therefore became a target of the South African government.

I had long ago come to the conclusion that there was no road to freedom except via the route of self-sacrifice, but nothing could have prepared me for what was to follow.

Three months after Nelson Mandela's release

from prison, I received a letter bomb hidden inside the pages of two religious magazines that had been posted from South Africa. In the bomb blast I lost both hands, one eye and had my eardrums shattered.

For the first three months I was as helpless as a newborn baby. People have asked me how I survived, and my only answer is that somehow, in the midst of the bombing, I felt that God was present. I also received so many messages of love and support from around the world that I was able to make my bombing redemptive - to bring life out of death, good out of evil.

Quite early on after the bomb I realised that if I was filled with hatred and desire for revenge I'd be a victim forever. If we have something done to us, we are victims. If we physically survive, we are survivors. Sadly, many people never travel any further than this. I did travel further, going from victim to survivor, to victor. To become a victor is to move from being an object of history to become a subject once more. That is not to say that I will not always grieve what I've lost, because I will permanently bear the marks of disfigurement. Yet I believe I've gained through this experience. I realise that I can be more of a priest with no hands than with two hands.

In 1992, I returned to South Africa to find a nation of Survivors, but a damaged nation. Everyone had a story - a truth - to tell. In my work I've developed a programme called the Healing of Memories. Our workshops explore the effects of South Africa's past at an emotional, psychological and spiritual level. I try to support those who have suffered as they struggle to have their stories recognised.

I haven't forgiven anyone, because I have no one to forgive. No one was charged with this crime, and so for me forgiveness is still an abstract concept. But if I knew that the people who sent my bomb were now in prison, then I'd happily unlock the gates - although I'd like to know that they weren't going to make any more bombs. I believe in restorative justice and I believe in reparation. So my attitude to the perpetrator is this: I'll forgive them, but since I'll never get my hands back, and will therefore always need someone to help me, they should pay that person's wages. Not as a condition of forgiveness, but as part of reparation and restitution.

The above story has been republished by kind permission of the "Forgiveness Project" *www.theforgivenessproject.com*

Matt Bower 2015

I was born 1977 in a well-to-do area. Up until the age of 10 it was a normal upbringing. My dad was a drinker and as a result my parents split up when I was about 11 years old. That was upsetting but what followed was abusive and traumatic.

My mom met a boyfriend when I was 12 years old and it was obvious I wasn't wanted. I went from being a son to being someone who it was okay to bully, emotionally abuse and use violence against.

By 14 I was self harming through despair & trauma.

My mum and sister used me as a punch bag. My sister later went to prison for armed robbery so that gives you an insight in how I stood no chance. When I used to get a chance to try & tell my mum I can't cope with her & her boyfriend & I am cutting my arm. She'd screw her face up & say what you going to do Matt. It wasn't the pain of being kicked and punched and hit with insults and arguments 4 reasons today I still don't know why, was it something to do with her boyfriend.

It was who was doing it, it was mum and sister my only family who was doing it.

I was diagnosed emotionally unstable and borderline personality disorder due to the trauma in the environment I grew up in.

When I was 23 I was sectioned under the mental health act 4 trying to kill myself for a number of reasons. I spent 8 months in a locked ward in an asylum. I used to really live dramatic incidents of abuse and violence every day 4 ten years plus which smashed any quality of life which may have been on offer.

I'm on 35 phyratic tablets a week for emotionally and instability, tranquillizers for trauma.

I used to go through extreme emotions for laughing then crying in the same breath and didn't know why I was laughing/crying for.

I'm 37 now and have done a lot of therapy and work on myself because I wanted to & had too.

> *One thing I tried to do is forgive my abusers,*
> *THIS MAKES THOSE MEMORIES*
> *REDUNDANT. IT TAKES THE POWER OUT*
> *OF THOSE MEMORIES.*
>
> *Forgiving heals the forgiver.*
>
> *Matt Bower 2015*

Seven questions to help you sort your life!

1. What's crucial to resolve in your life right now?
2. How is that impacting your life?
3. What do you know you've been doing that is preventing you from resolving this?
4. What has this cost you in the past?
5. How is this affecting you now?
6. What's going to happen in the future if you don't get this resolved/achieved?
7. What decision are you making inside yourself right now?

Abuse help coaching-
http://www.TomMcAbuseRecoveryCoach.co.uk

http://tinyurl.com/j34asab (TomMc ARC)

Chapter 7

Evolve - What will forgiving others do?

Do you want to take away the power to continue hurting you from your bullies and abusers?

The impact on your abusers or violators may be minimal unless you let them know that you have forgiven them.

If you communicate your forgiveness, they may or may not feel some remorse for their hurtful actions towards you.

Either way, do not concern yourself, as you are forgiving them for your sake rather than theirs.

The forgiveness will take away your pain and stop them from continuing to have power over you and make you suffer from the memories of your abuse.

Forgiving is not easy to do - you will have to take one small step at a time, repeating to yourself.

"I have forgiven and I am free from pain!"

"I have forgiven and I am free from pain!"

Repeat this over and over each day and you will be amazed at the results.

You will find that you can contemplate your past without feeling the pain and hurt that you have become accustomed to experiencing.

I will leave it to your imagination as to how you will feel when this happens.

I am sure you will feel that a heavy weight has been lifted and you will have a sense of freedom as never before.

You will be able to go forward and rebuild your life with a new sense of optimism.

You can at last allow gratitude, compassion and love into your life.

Once you forgive, you are taking control of your life and your mind; therefore, you will be able to create what comes into your life from now on.

254

Everyone on this planet is capable of making a success of their life despite all the obstacles that they encounter.

In fact, everyone has a different view and understanding of "success"

Successful people like athletes and golfers are always in "the zone" i.e. they are completely focused on winning. When you put yourself in the zone and give complete focus to the task you are likely to succeed and succeed easily.

I will relate a story about a colleague who had a habit of focusing on understanding the complete job before he started to work.

I will try to explain:- in our job we would get blueprints to work to, and when my colleague got his blueprints he would light up a cigarette (you were allowed to smoke at work in them bad old days) and spend about half an hour just study the drawings.

He very seldom made a mistake in his work because he had studied and planned ahead.

To be successful, you have to get in the zone and naturally feel and breathe as if you are already successful.

Visualize yourself as successful, how you look, how you feel, where you will be, who you will be with and even feel the atmosphere and smell the air.

Do this visualization frequently and your subconscious will go straight towards your success!

Believe that you are already worthy of success and expect it in everything you do.

Have confidence in your ability and your capacity to get up and continue no matter what the challenges hits you.

Expect success and it will be yours!

Success is like a Catch-22 situation in reverse, it will breed on itself, i.e. success will breed success. You will be able to build on one success after another when you remain positively confident of your abilities and skills.

Some people no matter how successful they are; do not get the full enjoyment out of their success and are unhappy and unfulfilled whatever the situation. Those individuals are missing the whole point of living your dream.

Success is not just wealth; it is enjoying the wealth and the good things that the wealth can bring.

If achieving success means that you have got to be in a constant state of worry or anxiety just to get where you want; then that success is senseless.

If you have continually to worry about your ability or skills to stay on top, you should consult your support team i.e. anyone you know as an expert in your field and get help from them.

One of the most fundamental needs in your life has got to be your desire to strive continually for success and achieve your goals and dreams. This, with your continued desire to improve your environment and the lot of your fellow human beings is an essential part of the attitude necessary for continued success and continued feeling of fulfillment in your life.

When this continual desire becomes natural, you will know that your subconscious mindset is anchored successfully in the right direction.

When you look elsewhere in this book at the meaning of success, you will realize that everybody's concept of success is inherently different. For some people their desire for success will not be satisfied until they are extremely rich financially, while for others success can mean happiness in the state they are in and with the material and health sources that they presently have.

What is your benchmark of success?

When you consider success there are many things you would have to take into account.

Look without fear on the prospects of failure!

You will meet failure perhaps many times but that does not mean complete failure, as failure should be viewed as the stepping stones towards success!

Failure is something that just happens to you and at one time or another to just about everybody.

It just puts you back at the beginning and when you show through strength of character, going forward and trying again then you will gain confidence in yourself and your abilities.

Failure is a chance to learn and to readjust your approach to whatever you are doing in such a way that the next time your chances of success are multiplied.

It is your responsibility to keep trying for success and not expect gratification of always getting to where you want the first time. If your goal was that easily achieved then you could consider that you may have set too low a goal and need to aim higher.

Do not expect to be perfect, at everything;

Nobody is perfect, and you will come up against problems and challenges to which you will not have the answer right away.

258

Believe in your subconscious to find the answer to all your problems.

There is always a way, all you need is belief in yourself and a passion for what you are doing, and you will reach your dreams.

All humans are completely different, have different strengths and weaknesses and no two people are the same.

We have each got our own special talents, whether we recognize them or not.

To strengthen self-belief I recommend you revisit you're "Toolbox" and review all the good things that you process within your character, your skills and your abilities.

Most people who write out their "Toolbox" in an honest way - not short changing themselves or over boosting - will feel quite proud when they read the good things that they possess in life.

When you seriously look at all the skills, talents and experiences that you have in your Toolbox you are bound to come up with a lot of different projects and undertakings that you are well equipped to tackle.

Make a list of the things that you love to do and cross-reference it with the skills and talents you have in your Toolbox and you will find it easy to pick out a job, a career or a business that is just right for you.

259

With a bit of brainstorming it will be possible to come up with a niche business idea that will have the potential of making you very successful.

There is a saying "thinking outside the box" and this is what it means, creative thinking that can propel you towards your dreams!

With belief in yourself and a little lateral thinking (thinking outside the box) you will surprise yourself and anybody that knows you, by your achievements.

Have you got specially skill or talent?

Everyone is unique and everyone has their own special skills and talents. Most of us are not completely aware of all of our skills and talents and until we looked deeply within our "Toolbox" we won't recognize the gifts we process and the uses we can make of those gifts.

Many talents and skills are easily recognizable such as singing, musicians, acting and specialist craft skills, especially as most people that posses them will be making use of those skills.

Other skills like teaching, artistry and the ability to put words together either as fiction or non-fiction can sometimes lay dormant and not be used for the benefit of those who possess them.

If you process some gift or skill that, with a bit of effort could be used for your benefit or you could use for the benefit of others, it is a disservice to yourself and to others not to use that skill.

If you have a skill or talent that you can pass on to someone else, maybe a skill you have been practicing in your work it is very rewarding to see someone else benefiting from your instructions.

Many people go through life unaware of the hidden skills and talents that they posses and this is sad because so many skills can give great pleasure when used effectively in our life.

As we grow older we can sometimes discover hidden talents and we never knew we had and it can give us great pleasure to pursue them sometimes as a full-time job or as a hobby.

Many people discover when they retire that they have an artistic skill and take up painting for instance. This can be hugely rewarding.

Everyone has something special that they know and that will benefit others, therefore it is very worthwhile to review your own skills and decide to do something with your special talents.

You may feel that you have nothing special to contribute, but everyone has some little bit of special information that is worthwhile and should be passed on to the rest of the world. If you don't share your special knowledge you are short changing yourself and everybody else.

You may have a talent that could change the world but if you don't use it or show it to the world then nothing will happen.

Have a go, let your light shine!

It would be dull and dreary world if we didn't have all the great talented people like singers, musicians and artists.

People like Ronan Keating, Mick Jagger, Paul McCarthy, Picasso, Monet or any modern artist, all make this world a more cheerful and happier place to be.

When you think of how many people have made such a great difference in the world sometimes just by their example and have helped other people to change their lives in a fantastic way, it is truly wonderful.

We look at all the great athletes, especially the Paraplegics, who overcome enormous difficulties and create huge feats of heroism that show others who doubt themselves what the possibilities are.

All those people have inspired perhaps millions by their example, showing their great skills and talents.

I am sure you have some great skill that you can pass on to others and when you do this one little bit at a time you will find that life has been worthwhile and you will feel extremely fulfilled.

You can do it one step at a time and as you take each step the next one becomes much easier.

There is nothing quite like the feeling you get when you know you have added to someone's life and to the advancement of the human race.

There will be many times in your life when you will be faced with almost insurmountable obstacles and you will need great courage, persistence and determination to get over those obstacles.

Giving up will often seem like the most sensible thing to do, however I have just read about a gold miner who stopped after many months of hard work as the seam he was working on had reduced down to almost nothing.

He sold all his machinery and went back to town. However the man he sold out to employed a surveyor who discovered that the gold seam started off again about 3 foot from where he had stopped.

Success can be just within arm's length - you never can tell.

Have you got the character and integrity to succeed?

Unless you have the character, the possibility of achieving success will almost become non-existent. You can make money without character, but it will not be of any lasting value to you unless you have the right character and mindset.

Criminals can make lots of money but it is of no use to them because they lack character and integrity.

When you build character and self respect, you will be honoured, respected, loved and trusted.

One of the best ways to smooth your path towards success is to build respect and be trusted by everyone you meet.

Respect can only be gained in one way - to get respect you have to give respect!

Integrity of course means honesty, and to be a person of integrity you have to be completely honest, something that is not very easy to achieve.

Being honest, honest with yourself as well as everybody else takes courage, persistence and a great depth of character.

When you are honest, you will have nothing to hide, therefore, nothing to fear.

Having integrity means that you will do right by everybody and not cheat in order to succeed or climb higher in your job.

I know of one young lady who within a very short period in her employment went straight into management, principally because of her integrity and character.

She has always been an advocate of fair play towards her fellow workers, always supporting others in the struggle for their rights.

Her integrity is second to none thereby earning the trust and appreciation of her employers, consequently her fast rise through the ranks to management.

She has proved my maxim - always prove yourself first then negotiate for what you are worth!

As a parent, it should be part of your character and integrity to put your family first.

You may have great difficulty in trying to convince your wife/ husband or partner that it is necessary to do extra hours to pay your mortgage. All those things are necessary but always look realistically at your situation.

Family time is precious; do not exchange it for work time just because your employer insists that you put in extra time.

This situation I would safely guess accounts for more than 50% of the stress in marriages and partnerships.

.

Have confidence in your ability and your capacity to get up and continue no matter what challenges hit you.

We live in a world of instant gratification and most people expect to get everything they want without making any great effort. This is of course completely wrong as anything worthwhile is worth working and fighting for.

Everything is possible but it won't happen by magic!

"Your attitude determines your altitude!"

When your attitude is one of helpfulness and firstly looking to what you can do for others instead of what they can do for you, you are on a straight road to success.

Everyone is looking for the benefits they can receive from others so when you can show others the benefits you can give them they will be your friend for life.

Remember my quotation:-

"You have to give before you get!"

When you have positive belief in yourself and confidence in your abilities you are setting yourself a benchmark for success.

There will be times in your life when you will meet with small failures and undoubtedly will feel frustration and anger, this is the time to dig deeply into your self -belief and recognize your abilities and your courage to carry on.

Overcoming the barriers you meet on the way to success will boost your confidence and self belief.

There may be times when the going gets tough that you may look at some of your peers or famous people that you know with envy and think "why is it easy for them and so hard for me?"

Now this is what I call falling into "self pity" what Zig Ziglar called "Poor Little old me" attitude!

This is a Catch-22 situation, as the more you entertain this attitude the further down the road towards negativity and failure you will travel.

Instead, stick a grin on your face, with your head up high and meet whatever barriers are put in your way head on. You know you can do it, just keep going.

"Never give up" should be your motto!

When you are considering success review the times you have succeeded in the past and how you felt with that success.

The feeling of power and importance you experienced when success was in your hands. Make that feeling your energy boost when the job gets difficult and problems are presenting themselves as you work on your project or job.

Relive the euphoria of success as you plan each move forward. As you go through life and you plan each new project or embark upon each job in your career always use your principles of honesty and truthfulness, humanity and tolerance.

You will begin to live by the rules of peace!

Our principles and values influence our decisions in our lives and when we have a positive mindset positive things come into our lives.

You do not need to feel alone!

When you have the right attitude and are helpful and cooperative with others, you will never lack the support of people in your community. You will not be alone to face your problems, and you will find support and strength from many different directions.

All the great achievers during time have always been able to find people to do things that they have not been capable of doing and to move their projects forward.

Henry Ford is one great example, as he was a man with all the great ideas and always prepared to hand over to his engineers confidently expecting results.

As you go through life right from your beginning you have been receiving support, health and education from many sources, your parents, your teachers and even the friends you made on the way.

268

If you have been wise you will have taken heed of all the constructive and helpful advice that has been given to you and ignored all the destructive and degrading criticism that I'm sure you will have received as well.

Unfortunately we often hear parents and teachers tell young people that they are so dumb and useless that they will never achieve anything.

This is complete rubbish of course because no matter how we start out in life, no matter how unintelligent we may seem every one of us have got success encoded within our DNA.

No one has ever been created to be a failure!

If your friends deny you encouragement, dump them - they are not friends.

Religious leaders are usually beneficial in their contribution to everybody's life and are good means of support.

Just as you will benefit from the support of others, you too can then support many people that you meet who are finding it difficult on their way through life.

Coaches and mentors are of great value in supporting you on the road to success, as they will have travelled that road before you.

What are the options for fixing or erasing our past?

The past's activities cannot be fixed!

What happened yesterday cannot be fixed or changed.

When you forgive somebody who has abused you, it doesn't mean you are acquitting them from the blame of their activities; it implies you are liberating yourself from their capacity to keep on harming you!

The hurt from the past can continue returning to the present with the same power as when that hurt was caused in the first instant - the best way to dull the agony is to "forgive"!

When you forgive, you take away the capacity of your abusers to keep on harming you with the recollections of your mortification, indignation and sense of betrayal. Here is an Affirmation that I suggest you repeat every day -

> *I am a Unique Human Being. I am built on a firm foundation of Honesty and Truthfulness, Humanity and Tolerance. I accept full responsibility for my actions and by building on my foundations and self-belief I am making a success of my life.*
>
> *I am a complete person, matchless, intelligent, important, compassionate, healthy, balanced, joyful and abundant with all the good things of life.*

Say this affirmation every day (I recommend that you stand up as straight as possible in front of a mirror) and witness the results!

I recommend that you study the above affirmation and recognize the deeper meaning of each sentence - it is a template to leading your life in the most fulfilled way possible.

This affirmation will become embedded in your subconscious over time and will motivate you to become all contained therein.

No one in the world can lead your life for you – only you can do that!

I suggest that you reread this book many times as you will discover new inspiring information each time!

"Forgiveness is the fragrance that the violet sheds on the heel that has crushed it."
<u>Mark Twain</u>

May good luck, good health and prosperity follow you all the days of your life!

Your Coach and Author TomMc (John McManus)

Disclaimer

This is an important notice and all potential readers are urged to read this before using newsletters, courses, newsletters, bulletins, books and any information published by John McManus.

While I have worked hard to develop and refine this information, and have proven the principals and values stated in the my literature, I do not make any express or implied claims or guarantees that readers will achieve any personal or business success as a result of using the information contained therein.

I, John McManus, am not responsible for any success or failure that you or your business experiences as a result of using the information contained in my literature. All business activity involves an element of risk, and the responsibility of managing this risk falls to you. As such, you should only take risks that you can afford.

While care was taken to ensure the data contained in my literature was accurate and complete at the time of publishing. It may be possible that there may be data discrepancies and inaccuracies therein.

Similarly, the data supplied on my website or on any book, ebook or publication sold or given away free by me should not be treated as advice and is designed for informational and educational purposes and should be treated as an educational resource only. Members are free to use the information I publish, but as it depends on the individual effort and circumstances I will not guarantee the results. Information published by me should not be treated as advice.

You are solely responsible for the consequences of your use of this material.

John McManus has always been called Tom Mc by his friends!

Acknowledgments:

To: Mathew Bower for his courage and honesty to share his story.

To: "Frank" for his tenacity and strength of character demonstrated by the love he has extended to his own family despite the cruelty he endured in his childhood.

To: My many clients in the "Shelter" who have taught me as much wisdom, if not more than I have taught them.

To: The *"Forgiveness Project"*
www.theforgivenessproject.com for their kind
permission to publish the stories in this book.

TomMc (John McManus)

http://www.tommcabuserecoverycoach.co.uk

tommc@tommcabuesrecoverycoach.co.uk

****

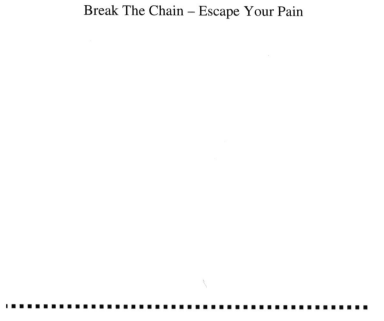

****

****

****

****

****

Printed in Great Britain
by Amazon